MW00655591

Ransacking the Closet

Yvonne Zipter

Spinsters Ink
Duluth

First edition
10-9-8-7-6-5-4-3-2

Spinsters Ink
32 E. First St., #330
Duluth, MN 55802-2002

Cover Design by Jill Walz and Barbara Richied

Production by:		
	Lindy Askelin	Carolyn Law
	Melanie Cockrell	Lori Loughney
	Patty Delaney	Jami Snyder
	Helen Dooley	Jean Sramek
	Joan Drury	Liz Tufte
	Emily Gould	Lee Ann Villella
	Kelly Kager	Nancy Walker

Library of Congress Cataloging-in-Publication Data
Zipter, Yvonne, 1954–
Ransacking the closet / Yvonne Zipter. —1st ed.
p. cm.
ISBN 1-883523-06-0 (acid-free paper) : $9.95
1. Lesbians—United States—Humor. I. Title.
PN6231.L43Z57 1995
814' .54—dc20 94-46130
CIP

Printed in the U.S.A. on acid-free recycled paper

Acknowledgments

Parts of this book were written at the Ragdale Foundation's artists colony in Lake Forest, Ilinois; I am deeply grateful to them for allowing me to make use of their incredible space—thanks especially to Mike and Deb for all their support and for making me feel at home.

An Illinois Arts Council fellowship grant provided partial funding for this work.

Portions of these essays have appeared previously in one or more of the following publications: *Baltimore Gay News; The Bridge; Couples: A Gay and Lesbian Newsletter on Coupling; In Step; Outlines; Partners: Newsletter for Gay and Lesbian Couples; Philadelphia Gay News; Phoenix Resource; The Washington Blade; The Weekly News;* and *The Windy City Times.*

Also by the author:

Diamonds Are a Dyke's Best Friend: Reflections, Reminiscences, and Reports from the Field on the Lesbian National Pastime

The Patience of Metal (poetry)

For Kathleen A. Forde,
the one I was waiting for all along

Contents

Preface:

A Deluge Of Dykes

If you don't already know it, you will come to understand during the course of this book that lesbians as a "people" are not like any other group of folks on earth. Our identity as a group does not arise from the fact that we all have names ending in "opoulos" or "mann" or that we all consume ale and kidney pie—and like it. Nevertheless, a large lesbian gathering can rarely be mistaken for anything else. Maybe the excessive amount of politically correct lingo riding the conversational currents is what sets us apart. Maybe it's a noticeable shift in the ratio of leg and underarm hair to head hair. Maybe it's the fact that almost no one is wearing lipstick and those who are have often accessorized with combat boots. Or perhaps it's the number of "children within" who are freely running about in thirty-plus-year-old bodies. Whatever that *je ne sais quoi* is that identifies a mess o' lesbians as lesbians, it seems clear to anyone who has ever found themselves at an Indigo Girls concert in the midst of the dozens of salivating women amorously flinging their delicate undergarments onto the stage that lesbians en masse are decidedly unique.

Given the distinct flavor of lesbians in community, it doesn't seem right to me to refer to us ever so mundanely as "a group of lesbians" or a crowd or a bunch. I want a word as vibrant and extraordinary as we are, a word that captures the essence of lesbians in the aggregate. So I spent a little quality time with my dear thesaurus—which, in case you were wondering, is one of the three books *I* would want with me on a desert island, along with a cooking-in-the-wild book and a tome on boat building. But to return to the topic at hand. . . .

Checking under the word "assemblage," I found the synonyms for "group"—"crew," "band," "throng," and "horde" —were boring. I did pause on the word "army," pondering how the phrase "An army of lesbians" reminded me of the old slogan "An army of lovers cannot lose." Ultimately, though, it rubbed my peacenik self the wrong way. Besides, how would we ever agree on what uniform to wear?

I proceeded from there to the sections on animals. I hesitated: How would lesbians feel about being associated with what we human types condescendingly refer to as the "lower life forms"? Would heated debates on evolution replace debates on S/M as a favorite lesbian pastime? What would the PC position be? At last I decided that I, for one, am proud of my ape roots—if we could all only be like Koko, the sign-language-speaking gorilla, and her kitten, this world would be a better place—and I forged ahead in my search, impervious to the potential slings and arrows of outrageous lesbians.

In so doing, I discovered biologists, or whoever it is that thinks up these group names, have a whimsical bent. Witness: a clowder of cats, a pod of seals, a gam of whales, a skein of geese (in flight), a watch of nightingales. As these terms seemed a bit too obscure to catch on, I decided to eliminate those as well. Others I rejected for not projecting lesbians in a flattering light: a sloth of bears—too lazy; a skulk of foxes—too sneaky; a plague of locusts—well, no sense in perpetuating our already bad press. "A charm of finches" is kind of, well, charming, but it reminds me of a chintzy trinket on a chain, causing my feminist hackles to rise. My favorite—"a murmuration of starlings"—sounds more like an appellation for a one-on-one thing than a rather large group thing. But maybe I'm merely being provincial in rejecting this appellation for such a reason. Be that as it may, I just felt it didn't really capture the essence I had in mind.

Ultimately failed by my thesaurus, then, I decided I would have to find a word of my own to claim especially for lesbians. Hey, Mary Daly does this sort of thing all the time—and just because I can never understand what the hell she's talking about doesn't mean I can't emulate her. In any case, here are the candidates I would offer to you:

A dapple of dykes. This construction evokes our diversity, and incidentally, is reminiscent of mares, for all of you who were "horse crazy" as prepubescent girls—a phenomenon whose implications, frankly, I don't want to examine too closely.

A jostle of lesbians. Jostle—"to drive or force . . . to

unsettle, disturb"—captures our struggle for acceptance and visibility.

A bristle of lesbians. Bristle—"to be visibly roused or stirred"—is appropriate on a number of levels. To mention but one of the PG-rated examples, there is the prickly nature of lesbian politics.

A burst of lesbians. I love the way this resonates with Audre Lorde's *A Burst of Light.* But does it represent us? Judge for yourself: "to issue forth suddenly and forcibly, as from confinement or through an obstacle; to give sudden expression to; to become visible, audible, evident." Now use it in a sentence:

"Nothing makes my heart soar like a burst of lesbians."

Introduction:

This Could Be The Start Of Something

When I became a columnist in 1985 for the new Chicago gay and lesbian newspaper, *The Windy City Times,* I took my job very seriously. I wanted to be the lesbian Anna Quindlen, probing the thorny issues that confront our community and standing for truth, justice, and the lesbian way. But then something weird happened. Like the Incredible Hulk turning green and reducing his clothing to neat tatters right before your very eyes, I metamorphosed into more of, like, a lesbian Andy Rooney (which comes up "Gooney" in my computer spellchecker). That's right: the lesbian Andy Rooney. Only less whiny. And more attractive. And funny. Before I knew what was happening to me, I found myself slipping from addressing the huge, weighty areas of a homosexual existence into commentaries on the little things of daily lesbian life—and finding the humor lodged there, like a poppy seed in your teeth.

I'm not quite sure why this transformation occurred. Maybe it was some deeply buried comic imprint rising to the surface—a sort of getting in touch with my inner clown. I do know, at least, that such an imprint existed, because not long ago I remembered I had been humor editor of my junior high newspaper, where my sense of humor had already put me in the midst of controversy. What transpired was this: I wanted to reprint a story handed down to me by my grandmother about a young gentleman whose gift of gloves to a young lady gets mixed up in the delivery process with his sister's purchase of bloomers—with which is enclosed a note from the young man, referring to the gloves. Oh, the merry mayhem! It included phrases such as "I chose these because I think you need them, as I have noticed you are not in the habit of wearing them when you go out in the evening," and "They are a very delicate color, but the lady I bought them from showed me a pair she had been wearing for three weeks and they were hardly soiled." The story cracked me up, big time. My elders, however, interceded: the story, they declared, was too risqué.

Or maybe what caused me to metamorphose was the fact that Reagan had recently been reelected. As Molly Ivins figures it (in her book, *Molly Ivins Can't Say That, Can She?),* the Reagan administration could "not only be endured, it can be laughed at. Actually, you have two other choices. You could cry or you could throw up. But crying and throwing up are bad for you, so you might as well laugh." The Reagan years were an especially bad time to be a lesbian. So when the going got tough, I got silly, reminding all of us about the fun—and funny—parts of being a lesbian in the right-wing eighties. Though I don't think I understood it as such at the time, I think what I was trying to do—in the face of so many who would have wished us to believe otherwise—was to reinforce what a normal, regular, and yet goofy and wonderful thing it is to be part of the diverse and incredible culture constructed by lesbians.

Whatever the cause of my shift from high drama to low comedy, it was a role I grew increasingly comfortable with. Drawing examples from my own experiences as well as my friends' experiences with and within lesbian culture, I somehow managed to create a loving picture of contemporary lesbian life—a picture otherwise easily lost in all of the antigay rhetoric, rhetoric which was made worse in some way because lesbians, even in this negative context, were often barely acknowledged. Hey, if we lesbians are at fault for the downfall of the nuclear family and decency, we'd at least like to get a little credit for it! As a consequence of this ongoing sense of erasure magically coupled with blame, lesbians—and gay men—took some sustenance from my self-loving, fun-loving words, stopping me in parking lots or writing me letters to tell me so. In my rambling ironic self-portraits, other lesbians seemed to recognize themselves and their own lives. Occasionally, I even seem to have inadvertently stumbled into descriptions of experiences universal to the human condition because a few brave nonqueers were chuckling right along with us.

Remember the old saw, "Don't laugh—it'll only encourage her"? Well, it's true. Thus encouraged by my readers, I continue to document my slightly warped perspective of gay and lesbian life in these United States in my column, which was initially titled "A View from the Inside," and then became "Inside Out" when I switched papers (from *The Windy City Times* to *Outlines)* in Chicago. It is from these columns that this book has sprung forth. Regular readers of my work may recognize bits and lines and even whole columns incorporated into these essays. I can't bear to throw anything away. Just ask my lover, who has to put up with the shells I collected in Florida in 1978, beer bottle labels I one day hope to use in a decoupage project, a crocheted pig my mother made, my grandfather's hat, and on and on and on. Although some of the material herein is recycled—in the best sense of the word, I hope—much of it is also new and fresh, the kind of fresh where someone gets her face slapped.

The chapter on sex, "Here At The Grand Coulee Dental Dam," for example, is entirely new, as I have never before been brave or foolish enough to tackle that terrifying subject. "Adventures In TherapyLand" is also heretofore unseen material. I have been collecting data for that one for years, but it took me a while to work through issues I was having with making light of the therapeutic process. And let's face it, making fun of one's therapist while currently engaged in therapy could, conceivably, have a detrimental effect on the outcome.

In contrast, not much of the chapter on dating, "Dates, Nuts, And Serial TV," is current material, as I haven't done any "research" in that area since 1987. And my girlfriend would like to keep it that way. Frankly, so would I, the reasons for which will become eminently clear to you upon reading the chapter. The same can be said for "How To Spell Lover With An X."

Other chapters—such as "Who Holds The Purse Strings When No One Owns A Purse?"—are a lovely mélange of preprocessed material and fresh stuff, sort of like a Betty Crocker cake mix. The latter assessment also applies to "Which One Of You Is The Mother?" and "The Marrying Kind," although in the former case I had to quell the urge, in spite of my irreproachable lack of bias, to wax rhapsodic about the incredible beauty and superior intelligence of my "niece" and "nephew," the outstanding offspring of my dearest friends. Fascinating though I knew this material would be to all and sundry, I resisted the temptation out of concern for our dwindling forest resources. In the case of "The Marrying Kind," I again find myself with no shortage of material. In this instance, though, it is my girlfriend's eyeballs rolling heavenward rather than environmental consciousness that has prevented me from relating, for example, my highly developed method for avoiding extrarelational dalliances: to begin with, do not, under any circumstances, offer to teach the object of your infatuation how to do a self-breast exam—this could only, I would think, serve to fan the flames higher.

Another au courant sort of chapter would be my exploration of the unnatural coupling of lesbians and television, "What The Nielsons Don't Know (And We'd Rather Not Admit)." Hours of painstaking research were spent sitting on the couch watching sitcoms so that you, the reader, could benefit from updated versions of material I wrote a long, long time ago.

As for the title chapter, "Ransacking The Closet," which connotes my chaotic style of demystifying "the lesbian lifestyle," I have sifted through all of my shades of coming out stories over the years and distilled them down to a funky nugget—a sort of Herbal Essence of lesbian self-outing tales, only with a lot less funeral parlor smell. Remember that shampoo? Exactly what was supposed to be so attractive about reeking like a raft of memorial wreaths? Unless you spill your patchouli oil on this book, I think I can guarantee that "Ransacking The Closet" will be much less odiferous.

Anyway, as this smattering of allusions to what's in the book may tell you, the parts of lesbian culture and life in general that I tend to be most interested in are interpersonal relationships, whether with lovers, ex-lovers, families—biological and otherwise—or therapists. All of these relationships confound me on some level. I have found comfort in sharing this confusion with others. I hope you find comfort in reading it. Or, if not, that you at least laugh till your sides hurt. And if you do laugh, tell me about it at your own risk, bearing in mind it will only encourage me.

Yvonne Zipter
Chicago, Illinois
September 1994

The Lesbian Mystique

How many lesbians does it take to make a mystique? Eight: one to wear the flannels and cords, one to wear the leathers, one to write the scholarly papers, one to nurture the women-only space, one to run the corporate world, one to wield the gym bag, one to organize the rallies and protests, and one to blend right in with all the other neighbors on the block.

Okay: so it's not very funny—but I *did* write it myself. Like, if I didn't tell you, you'd think Letterman's people were now writing for me. And it *does* get my point across. Which is what? you might rightfully ask.

It's this: well, really, it's impossible to say exactly what a lesbian is (or isn't, for that matter) beyond the obvious, which is that she is a woman who has sex with other women—which isn't all that obvious unless you happen to be there with her in whatever place she happens to be making her amorous statement, so to speak. And this definition isn't even particularly correct—what about, for instance, your celibate lesbians? I could go on, but it is this difficulty of definition that lends substance to the lesbian mystique, the air of mystery surrounding our lives—that and because decades of persecution have prompted many of us to be a little less than open about what people persist in calling "our lifestyle." I keep expecting Robin Leach to show up on my doorstep with a film crew and Dionne Warwick.

You can tell we have a mystique because so many people find us just so darn *interesting*. For instance, there's Oprah, Phil, Geraldo, and the gang, who are always putting us on display like sideshow freaks; there are the men who buy those magazines with "the good articles" who seem to have developed a rich fantasy life around us; and there are the tabloids, which use speculation about who is among us and who is not to sell their papers—that's how interesting we are. And we're so mysterious that right-wingers are terrified of us—like UFOs: Unidentified Fag-like Objects.

Well I'm here to tell you: we ain't all that mysterious. We put our chaps on one leg at a time, just like everyone else. Just kidding—chaps don't even have legs, per se. But really, in many ways, lesbians *are* just like everyone else: we experience the same emotions for pretty much the same reasons, we go to work every day, pay mortgages and rents, do housework, go home for the holidays, go to the movies, and watch TV—although maybe we didn't watch "Cagney and Lacey" for quite the same reasons as your average housewife. Then again, maybe we did. . . .

This is not to say, however, that there are *no* differences. There are, in fact, many differences. And thank the goddess for that, the lesbian chauvinist in me says. Even so, on an everyday basis, most people wouldn't know they're talking to a lesbian when they're talking to me—unless, of course, I happen to have turned on the flashing neon sign imbedded in my forehead reading "lesbian" or I'm necking with my girlfriend while they speak. But what I really meant to say was: most people wouldn't know about me *who aren't gay or lesbian.* Because even without blatant visual cues, we homos have a way of picking one another out, even across a crowded shopping mall or at the deli counter at the 7-11. We call this ability "gaydar" ("gay radar," for the etymologically impaired). But then the question comes up, if we look so much like everyone else, how does this gaydar stuff work? To echo Spike Lee in those Nike commercials, Is it the shoes?

Why yes, Spike, it is the shoes—among other things. The thing is, you can't just pick any one thing that identifies someone as a lesbian—unless it's that "I'm not a lesbian but my lover is" t-shirt. It's the whole gestalt, ranging from footwear to clothing to accessories to haircuts to carriage to a certain *je ne sais quoi.* But, for the sake of Spike, let's start with the shoes.

There was a time, many moons ago, when I would have said Reeboks were yuppie shoes. Then there was another time—my birthday party, 1987, to be exact—when I realized Reeboks, especially in black, were *dyke* shoes. It was right after we played pin the tail on the dyke (rock 'n roller Tret Fure, if memory serves me correctly), or was it after that rousing round of drop the tampon in the bottle? Anyway, a burst of five lesbians happened to be standing casually in a haphazard line—four had on black Reeboks, the fifth one wore yellow. For a while there, so many lesbians were shod with the R-shoes that I suspected one could truthfully say, "Ye shall know them by their feet." I even envisioned Madison Avenue constructing entire ad campaigns pitched at lesbians: a photo of a woman, for instance, resplendent in tie, tails, and black Reeboks. Caption: "Dyke Formal Wear." Or, a four-color ad to run in *Common Lives/Lesbian Lives* with a line of women all wearing Reeboks, shown from the calf down only, a flyer for k. d. lang or Michigan at their feet. Headline: "No More Ugly Dyke Lines," with one of those red circles with the slash through the middle, right over a workboot.

Anyway, now I'm singing a different tune, "Where have all the Reeboks gone?" These days, dykes everywhere seem to be clomping around in Doc Martens: those heavy-duty leather numbers that weigh about ten pounds each. With their giant corrugated rubbery soles, they're the elevator shoes of the nineties. Oh sure, between the weight and the extra height, you may have a gait bearing an uncanny resemblance to that of Frankenstein, but you'll be thanking your lucky stars you've got your Doc Martens on next time you're out in a drifting boat looking for an anchor. And this is not to say they're not attractive shoes, in their own Third Reichian sort of way, but my girlfriend's father did once say, "If we had made you wear shoes like that when you were a kid, you would've cried." Now, personally, it's just the price of those things that brings tears to my eyes. Lesbians are far from being the only folks to wear Doc Martens, of course, but doesn't it seem obvious they were designed specifically with lesbians in mind? No-nonsense shoes for no-nonsense women: I'd say that makes them lesbian shoes—either that or nun shoes, although the two categories are not necessarily mutually exclusive.

Really, the truth is, there is no such thing as lesbian clothing. But if you spot some woman taking long strides down the frozen foods aisle—unencumbered by a purse—whose attire makes her appear equally ready to embark on a hike or sit at a hotline switchboard for several hours, chances are, you're looking at a dyke, honey. It is at this point that my girlfriend and I turn to each other with raised eyebrows (one each) and a smile (one each) and say, "Dit-da-dit?" our code word for "lesbian"—one of many such appellations gleaned from lesbian folksinger Alix Dobkin's internationally compiled list. (Among other favorites: "she bats on our team"; "she's a member of the church"; and "vagitarian.")

Hairstyles come into play with gaydar as well. Used to be some sort of buzz cut guaranteed you a genuine lesbian. But that was before Sinead O'Connor came and mucked things up. Now the best you can do is look for a hairstyle with a wash-and-wear quality, whether long or short. Most lesbians, in my experience, don't like to spend a lot of time messing with their do. Although I must point out, somewhat admiringly, that along with power lunching, many corporate dykes have acquired skill with a curling iron. In my own hairstyling endeavors, I couldn't even successfully wield a round brush and a blow drier without incorporating the brush into the hairstyle. I can't imagine bringing something you could steam vegetables with that close to my head. My hair would probably go up in flames—do you think that's how Sinead got her start?

Even with knowledge of all these elements, I've gotta say gaydar just isn't what it used to be. I blame this on two things: *(1)* more lesbians have been getting in touch with their feminine side, and, mostly, *(2)* heteros are stealing all our best stuff. We can't keep anything nice around here!

Gay men, of course, were targets of this sort of theft long before lesbians were. Who do you think first breached the pastel clothing barrier for men? But this experience, until relatively recently, had not been shared by us less trendsetting lesbians. The tide has turned, however, and decidedly lesbian "stuff" has suspiciously been showing up in the mainstream.

If I were filing a police report, I would have to include the following:

Butch hair cuts. Sinead's not the only nonqueer out there doing it, either. In the old days, you'd see a woman walking down the street looking like she just came from the barber (not beauty) shop, and, on passing one another, you might have exchanged knowing glances. These days, chances are only one of you will be knowing.

Fanny packs. I'm not a fashion expert so I may be mistaken about this, but I think fanny packs were originally conceived of as biking gear. However, it was lesbians—those gals on the go—who first adapted the fanny pack as a sort of butch purse. Or maybe it was gay men first, with lesbians a close second. Anyway, that fanny packs have been perceived as a homosexual thing is not merely the product of my own little, but admittedly vivid, imagination: the mother of a friend of mine once enquired of her lesbian offspring whether you could tell who was gay by who was wearing a fanny pack. Well, certainly not anymore, Mrs. McGillicutty: everybody and anybody can now be seen adorned—festooned, if you will—with fanny packs of every size, material, and color imaginable. Accessories may still make the outfit but they don't make the queer.

Sensible shoes. Our invention too—well, not that we invented the shoes, mind you, but we came up with the concept of actually wearing them on a regular basis, not just on the tennis court. Now you go downtown, any city, and what do you see? Countless women, dressed for success, shod in Nikes or whatever. Oh sure, maybe once in the confines of their offices these same women slip on some heels, but even those aren't as death-defyingly high as they once were. Moreover, *elderly* women are switching their everyday foot apparel to tennis shoes. At my grandmother's retirement home, there are women who only recently wouldn't be caught dead in anything more casual than open-toed wedgies who are now wearing sneakers with Velcro closures—I know because I've seen them sticking out from their smart little polyester pant suits.

The grunge look. Second-hand-store attire, flannel shirts, jeans, big shoes, a general lack of concern for outward signs of care in grooming: Invented by a bunch of hip young over-caffeinated kids in Seattle? Or herbal-tea-drinking lesbians in the seventies? You tell me who was there first with this look.

Uneven numbers of earrings. What can I say? You'd think Melissa of the ill-fated show *thirtysomething* (a misdirected hetero if ever there was one) invented this fashion statement. Pretty much ever since pinkie rings went out of vogue in the lesbian community as a "fashion" statement (or maybe even before then), our secret sign to one another has been if you wear just one earring on the right (you can't get much more uneven than that!), others will know you're gay. Or is it the left side? I always did get confused. Actually, I think it's that very point of confusion that prompted so many of us to adopt, instead, the three-earring system—which was working just fine until Melissa gummed up the works.

The lesbian label. Apparently our *je ne sais quoi* has grown so popular that now women who aren't even lesbians call themselves lesbians—you know who I mean: those lesbians who sleep with men. It's very flattering that they want people to think they are lesbians, and I do think people should be able to define themselves in any way they like, but there already exists a perfectly good word for lesbians who sleep with men: "bisexual." Is nothing sacred?

But as I mentioned earlier, not all of our problems with the breakdown of gaydar can be blamed on thefts by heteros and bi's; some of it is our own darn fault. As a victim of faulty gaydar, though, this is a bit of a sensitive issue for me. The problem for me, in a nutshell, is that people who should be raising their eyebrows at me in a knowing fashion are now passing me by with nary a twitch of furry brow or a glimmer of appraising eye. I thought at first this was because we lesbians—media whores that we've become of late—had simply grown blasé about seeing other dykes, whatever the context. But then one day, when an unknown baby dyke grinned broadly at my girlfriend Kathy and didn't so much as flicker an eyelash at *moi,* it began to dawn on me that was not the case at all. "She didn't recognize you as a lesbian," Kath observed, a tremor of angst in her voice. Either that, or I just wasn't her type, I thought. It is Kathy's disturbing hypothesis, though, that has been confirmed to be true: a young gay man recently asserted to Kathy, in reference to me, "She doesn't look like a lesbian."

Ladies and gentleman, it would seem that I—me, the

Lesbian Pride Poster Child—have been passing. What kind of a topsy turvy world is this when a gal who wears sensible shoes, no makeup, and an uneven number of earrings can't even be recognized as a lesbian? I blame this on—along with the aforementioned purloined items—my voluptuous locks, which make me look like a girlie girl even though it is the requisite low-maintenance do—not that there's anything wrong with that. Some of my best friends are lipstick lesbians.

If you ever bore witness to my purple tail, or, for that matter, my name and photograph on this book! you would know I am not the sort who goes in much for the invisibility thing. Plus which, I miss getting to have "a moment" with a total stranger in the power tool department at Sears. I cannot presume to speak for all the other long-haired lesbians who may be enduring a fate similar to mine, but personally, I have decided, gaydar be damned: I'm gettin' me some freedom rings, family-size pink triangles for every outfit, and a snappy new easy-to-recognize bumper sticker for the car. I am no longer trusting my significant eye contact across a crowded potato bin to something as flawed as gaydar. If I were a braver woman, I would have entwined women symbols tattooed on some prominent place on my body. However, given that I am needle phobic, I have decided instead just to wear my Dykes to Watch Out For t-shirt twenty-four hours a day, seven days a week. Well, maybe I'll take it off once in a while to wash it; otherwise, I'll be getting significant eye contact of a different nature entirely. It might not hurt, either, to get a kickass black leather jacket and some Doc Martens boots. It occurs to me, though, that this attire must get awfully hot in the summer. I suspect the tough-girl dyke image I am hoping to create here would not be enhanced by my fainting like some sort of weird hybrid of Southern belle and biker chic. "I don't know nothin' 'bout birthin' no Harleys." WHOMP.

The truth is, gaydar was *never* exactly foolproof—if it was, we never would have had to "invent" lesbian bars, coffeehouses, music festivals, bookstores, and softball leagues. We would have gone on indefinitely raising our eyebrows at one another until eventually we mutated into a race of women with one eyebrow genetically higher than the other.

In any case, even now, without the patented lesbian highbrow, there's more to the quintessential lesbian than what she wears or how she cuts her hair—or whether the area directly over her eyes is especially limber. For one thing, we lesbians seem to have a peculiar (if not unique) relationship to time. I am talking, of course, about what is "affectionately" known as "Dyke Standard Time." (Did you remember to set your clocks back?) In layperson's terms, Dyke Standard Time means: nothing ever starts on time in the entire realm of the lesbian community. If a concert or program flyer advertises an 8 p.m. starting time, you can figure things won't really get going until 8:30 at the earliest. If you throw a party—*even a dinner party*—and no one is there at the time proposed on the invitation, don't worry: it's just DST. Frankly, when a gal joins up with the lesbians, I think it would be useful if she were issued a time conversion chart so she could easily translate the announced time of an event into the *actual* starting time. Unfortunately, no one has had the time to figure out what the conversion equation is, and the phrase "Dyke Standard Time," by now a time-worn joke, has yet to go out of date.

And speaking as someone who was born two weeks

late but has been early ever since, I find it maddening how chronically tardy dykes are. Despairing of anyone ever being on time, I have often tried—yes, tried—to be late myself. And even then, after watering the plants, straightening up the house, calling my grandmother—even then, I'm often the first one there, whether it's a program at the bookstore, dinner with friends, a volleyball game, a party—whatever. The time-change conversion factor remains a mystery to me, you see. Therefore, while contemplating my dilemma, I thought perhaps if I tried to *understand* the overdue lesbian I would at least be able to reconcile myself to being ahead of, if not my time, then everyone else's time. Here's what I came up with.

They were late because:

1. *They were making love.* Especially when they're newly in love, lesbians have a tendency to get carried away. What starts out as a kiss can end up as—well, you know. For lesbians in love, time is not only not of the essence, it's not even of the slightest interest.

2. *They were fighting.* If lesbians don't make love right before going out, it could be because they were fighting. This is probably not all that common among the newly in love, but give them a few months, boy, and. . . . At first, you don't care—heck you don't even notice—that she always squeezes the toothpaste from the middle or puts the toilet paper on the holder the "wrong" way, but as all that passion begins to wear you down a little (sleep deprivation will do that), well, one can get a might testy. And don't think she hasn't noticed, either, that you leave your shoes right in the middle of the floor where somebody could trip over them.

3. They made love after fighting. Ah, the ol' "kiss and make up" of movie fame . . . but, hey, they were obviously basing those scripts on something—although probably not lesbians. But that's only a guess.

4. They couldn't figure out whose Doc Martens were whose—or Birkenstocks, if we're talking crunchy dyke. Now, apparently, we can also add those Teva sandals to the list. You know what I mean, those shoes which are basically high-tech flip-flops, with a price to match their relatively greater technical attributes—namely, a Velcro strap around the ankle, presumably offering you less flop to your flip-flop.

5. They were waiting to see if a better offer came along. It seems like lesbians are unwilling to make a commitment—even to come to a party, as a friend pointed out. Lesbians never seem sure of what they want to do. And the confusion is compounded doubly if we're talking about a couple. It's as if they're waiting for divine inspiration. Or playing chicken with time.

6. They couldn't decide who should drive. In a heterosexual relationship (although this is changing a bit these days), men generally drive. But with lesbians, who's driving, unless one of them doesn't have a car, is never really clear. Any number of factors can come into play in making this decision—who drove last, who has gas in her car, who's closer to the point of destination, who's feeling most butch today, who's least likely to get pulled over by the cops for delinquent tickets when she takes the car out of the garage, etc. Hence the potential for seemingly endless conversation in making this decision.

7. They have to find out which of their ex-lovers will be there. For a community as big as Chicago, when you've just had a painful or difficult break-up (and how many of them aren't?), it's amazing how small the community becomes. To avoid dramatic scenes, feelings of discomfort, or nasty surprises, lesbians will sometimes make innumerable phone calls to try to determine if an ex has plans to attend the event in question, if the ex's new lover will be there, et cetera. These questions can sometimes involve high-level negotiations that make summit meetings look like "What's My Line" or "I've Got a Secret." Tell them what they'll be playing for tonight, Don Pardo. . . .

8. They've misplaced a cummerbund, a knee pad, the mousse. In the old days, all a self-respecting dyke needed to do before going out was throw on a pair of cords or jeans and a flannel shirt. But dykes today have a tendency to be dressed for the occasion down to the last detail. If it's an athletic activity, they've got all the right clothing and equipment. If it's a night out at the flashy women's dance bar in town, the look is completely coordinated, from accessories to hair. But as fastidious as dykes today can be about their appearances, they always seem to be misplacing something—two minutes after they're supposed to be out the door.

9. They forgot to check their calendars. I dunno—maybe straight folks and gay men are this way too—but I don't know one lesbian who doesn't keep track of all of her social engagements and extracurricular commitments on a calendar. "Let me check my calendar" could be the start of the lesbian national anthem. Lesbians—at least the ones I know—are the busiest darn bunch of folks. Perhaps they've heard that mini-poem of mine: "The social butterfly / never lands / on the wall flower."

10. They hate to be the first one there. No, scratch that one—because *(a)* half the community knows they couldn't possibly be the first one there, because I'll be there before them, and *(b)* after years of being the first one there, I've definitely grown to hate it—and I still can't manage to be late. I guess it's just, as a Capricorn and a first-born, I've felt responsible for making my mother wait those fourteen days right there at the beginning and have been overcompensating ever since. This makes for some maddening moments in our household, given that my girlfriend is substantially less driven by fear of tardiness than I am. I have, in fact, on numerous occasions accused her of trying to do me in with her much more tortoise-like approach to getting ready, which stands in stark contrast to my more hare-like tendencies.

Still, I suspect "the late Yvonne Zipter" probably won't ring true even when I'm dead. That's why I've told my girlfriend that what I'd like on my tombstone is, simply, "xyz." Pithy and to the point—just my style.

But let's not shilly-shally over the lateness thing. Time to move on to another lesbian topic: pets. Oh, I don't mean pets *per se,* of course, but the roles they've played in the lesbian community—King Lear, Macbeth, Othello. Rim shot. Sorry, I couldn't help myself.

Actually, pets are frequently the most consistent companions a lesbian may have, what with moving to San Francisco or wherever and breaking up with someone every other month. I don't mean to imply all lesbians are animal lovers. And even among those who do harbor feelings of affection for our little furry friends, there is many a species-ist bias.

The most common among these, of course, are the dog-lovers versus the cat-lovers. So fervent are these two camps in their commitments to their respective critters that battle lines have been drawn, each group insisting their four-legged friend is the best. While at base the arguments are all pretty subjective, on the surface they range around such "objective" things as grooming proclivities, "rest room" requirements, intelligence, obedience, feeding habits, and so on. A classic example of the canine/feline split is when PC dykes claimed that cats were the PC animal of choice. Frankly, I never understood why—especially given that PC dykes are supposed to be vegetarians, and cats, unlike dogs, *must* have meat in their diets or they will go blind. I read this in *TV Guide* several years ago so it must be true. This sort of PC bias in favor of cats, though, strikes me as being racist against canines—to paraphrase a woman at a workshop at Michigan one year, who felt she was being "racist against freshmen" (by which she meant "ageist," I guess), a phrase that has tickled my lover and me with its illogic ever since.

By now you are probably saying to yourself, "Oooh: those lesbians *are* an odd bunch: they have pets, sometimes they're late, sometimes they have short hair, sometimes long, and they wear *shoes,* for God's sake! No wonder they've suddenly become so fascinating." *Of course* you're not saying that—to yourself or anyone else. What you are saying is, "Hah! Lesbians sound just like everyone else." And that, my friends, is the heart of the mystery: How can a group of folks seem so much like everyone else and yet, somehow, be so quintessentially different in some indescribable way that makes people want to legislate that we shouldn't, for example, be allowed to raise our own children? If you read this thinking that *I,* the author, could explain the lesbian mystique, boy, were you barking up the wrong book. I mean, what do I look like to you—Jessica Fletcher? No way! To begin with, her hair is *much* shorter than mine. . . .

1,001 Dykes

Once you've decided you are, in fact, a lesbian, you might think all your big decisions are made. But you're not done yet. No: you still have to determine what *kind* of dyke you are. There are bar dykes and political dykes, S/M dykes and separatist dykes, jocks and femmes, lipstick lesbians and crunchy dykes, literary dykes and corporate dykes, butches and crystal-packin' mamas. The worst part is that most of these categories are not mutually exclusive, making the combinations and permutations rather daunting. You could, for instance, be a literary-separatist jock or a butch-political-bar dyke. Or, if you really set your mind to it, you could be a spiritual-S/M-political-lipstick jock—which would require a great deal of care in choosing an outfit. Personally, I'd like to meet a crunchy-S/M-literary femme. Does Birkenstock, for instance, even *make* a studded black leather sandal? Where *do* you shop for a black leather peasant skirt? And can any shade of lipstick really be considered "natural"?

There are, in fact, so many options available to the modern dyke that I think aptitude tests might be extremely helpful in sorting things out. I, for instance, have often struggled with the question of whether or not I'm a jock. My heart says "yes" but my shins say "no." To help resolve this dispute, I decided to take the following test.

How Much of a Jock Are You?

1. *My best slide is:*
   - *a.* Head first.
   - *b.* Feet first.
   - *c.* The waterslide at Santa's Village.
2. *I mostly prefer leather in:*
   - *a.* Balls and baseball mitts.
   - *b.* Mini-skirts.
   - *c.* Book covers.
3. *A "button hook" is:*
   - *a.* A type of football play.
   - *b.* A receptacle for storing spare buttons.
   - *c.* A device used to pull buttons through buttonholes on turn-of-the-century shoes.
4. *I play sports:*
   - *a.* For the physical challenge.
   - *b.* To get dates.
   - *c.* Only at gun point.
5. *The last pair of hightops I owned were:*
   - *a.* For basketball or some other sport.
   - *b.* Because they looked cool.
   - *c.* For ankle support when I was a toddler.

6. *What are you willing to sacrifice in the course of play?*
   a. Whatever it takes, no matter how great the hospital bill.
   b. No more than one limb.
   c. A small bruise on the upper thigh where no one will see it.

7. *I spend most of my reading time on:*
   a. Sporting goods catalogs.
   b. The sports page of the newspaper.
   c. Lesbian romances from Naiad.
   d. Artsy oversized books from contemporary fiction series.

8. *My favorite fields are:*
   a. Football and rugby.
   b. Softball
   c. Ones with wild daisies.
   d. Mrs.

9. *During the winter of 1994, what had you glued to the TV set?*
   a. The Olympics.
   b. Brady Bunch reruns.
   c. The latest installment of "Masterpiece Theater."

10. *In softball, when I bat I:*
    a. Hit the ball to wherever I want.
    b. Hit the ball.
    c. Hit on the catcher from the other team.

11. *My favorite Wilma is:*
    a. Wilma Rudolph.
    b. Wilma Flintstone.
    c. Wilma Mankiller.

12. *My favorite between-games snack is:*
a. Beef jerky and a beer.
b. A power bar and Gatorade.
c. A scone and a latté.

In scoring your answers, give yourself 1 point for every *a* answer, 2 points for every *b,* 3 points for every *c,* and 4 points for every *d.* If you scored under 14 points, you make Martina look like a wimp. If you were in the range of 15–21 points, you're in the dictionary under "jock." A score of 22–26 points means you could be a jock if you cared for your body either a little more or a little less. If you scored 27–31 points, only those scoring over 31 would ever think of you as a jock. And you lucky women who scored over 31 can be free of any anxiety over your status in the athletic world: you are definitely not jocks. Given that my own score of 27 indicates, as it turns out, that I'm not much of a jock, just what kind of a dyke am I?

In my younger days, when career choices were fewer for lesbians, I strove to be a bar dyke. Like jock, bar dyke is not a choice for the faint of heart. Being a bar dyke is a lot of hard work: the hours are bad, you're around hazardous materials, you're on your feet for hours at a time, you have to endure dangerous decibel levels, and, on top of all that, you have to deal pleasantly with the public. Bar dykes are essentially sales personnel: smiling, schmoozing, working the crowd, pouring on the charm, hoping to sell themselves to some comely lass.

Actually, when you're a bar dyke, your work begins at home, long before you casually saunter, just the way you rehearsed, into that dark denizen of damsels. There are the endless sessions of dance practice in front of the mirror, the shopping excursions to keep that wardrobe up to date, the ensemble planning, and the meticulous grooming, including cologne selection and hair styling. When I was a bar dyke, I started prep work hours before my midnightish ETA at the old watering hole by setting up the ironing board in front of the TV set so I could watch "Dance Fever" while I pressed my outfit and get psyched for disco-ing the night away. Coach Denny Tario (the host) delivered the before-game pep talk. Driving to the bar, I would be all atingle in anticipation of what the night might bring—which frequently was absolutely nothing. Unless, that is, you count as "something" sore feet, cigarette smoke in your hair, and a bruised ego. You might think a gal would get discouraged at this sort of metaphoric roughing up. Well I was. But like a quarterback who's just been sacked, I got right back out there the very next week—sometimes even the very next night.

Because, above all, a bar dyke is persistent. As an illustration of just *how* insanely persistent, I offer the following story. Shortly after moving from Manhattan to Lisle, Illinois (pop. 11,000—but it's right next to Naperville, which has a population of *40,000*, as the realtor encouragingly pointed out to me), life among the cornfields and corporate yuppies got to me. It got to me so bad, in fact, that I was determined to hit the bars in Chicago—forty-some miles away—in spite of the fact that I didn't own a car. Or rather, hit the bar, as I only knew of one in the whole city at that juncture in time. The main thing is: I had a plan. I would ride my bike the three miles to the train station in town, lock it up there, board the train, travel to the end of the line in Chicago, take a bus, and walk the remaining half mile to the bar—though I had *no* idea what kind of neighborhood I would be walking through at night. And even though, when it came time to hop on my bike that night, it was raining, and even though I didn't own any rain gear, did I let that stop me? No. There are just some things in life that you *have* to do, no matter how great the challenge, no matter how high the odds are against you, because they are things you believe in, dreams that must be fulfilled because they are at the core of your being. But to get back to going to the bar that night. . . . I was so desperate to see those of my own kind, I took a dry cleaning bag, cut arm and leg holes in it, and wore it like a poncho for my ride to the train station. I looked like a sack of produce wheeling through the sprayer section of your grocer's vegetable department.

In spite of my obvious diligence in the bar dyke trade, in my heart of hearts, I knew that wasn't me either. For one thing, I was never very proficient at some of this field's traditional activities—like shooting pool, making small talk, consuming alcohol, and cutting the rug. These days when my girlfriend and I go to a bar—about once every year or two, whether we need to or not—we fit in about as well as a couple of blondes in sombreros and sun dresses in Zacatecas. How far out of the scene are we now? Well, my girlfriend was hit on while I was at the espresso bar. She didn't realize it until five minutes later, and then, we were nearly trampled on the dance floor when the crowd spontaneously broke into something called "a line dance." The last time *I* did anything resembling a line dance was when we did the bunny hop at my grandparents' anniversary party in 1958—unless you count that game of red rover in 1966.

If the world of fleshly pursuits—that is, rugby and dancing, brought on by the conspicuous consumption of alcoholic beverages—had left me in the dust, I reasoned that perhaps more inner-oriented explorations would be my cup of tea. I came to New Age spirituality with an open heart—and a hefty dose of skepticism left over from my Christian upbringing, from which my favorite story had been the one in which that dude Tom refuses to believe it's Jesus until he touches the nail holes. Now *this* was a Bible story I could identify with. And though my child within jumps up and down at the idea of witches and goddesses and magical healing done with crystals, I am still way too Doubting Thomas–identified to really let go and throw myself into the whole thing. Try though I might, when I think witches, I think Elizabeth Montgomery, twitching her nose, and when I think goddesses, I think k. d. lang. For me, a ritual is eating frozen yogurt while we watch *Picket Fences* and the closest I get to a soulful connection with the invisible life force is team spirit. I'm afraid that if there's an earth mother in me, she's way too embarrassed to come out. My tarot cards lie orphaned in an unopened box.

Not discouraged at my failure to find a match between me and the goddess gang, I pressed on in the search for a niche of my own. Some options were so clearly wrong for me, though, that it didn't seem worthwhile to even try them out. For instance, S/M dyke: I just haven't got The Right Stuff for that line of work. As evidence of the truth of this, I put to you the following: *(1)* My neck is very tender and would chafe if I were to wear a dog collar. *(2)* I am tempted to seek out a medical professional for painkillers when I get a paper cut. *(3)* I don't have an immediate answer (as I suspect a *true* S/M babe would) when my girlfriend asks if they have clip-on nipple rings for those who aren't ready yet to make the commitment. And *(4)*, if I were truly *cut out* for S/M, I would have played rugby all those years ago when I had the chance.

In a continual effort to be a well-rounded dyke, I did decide to try the political thing. Oh sure, I've done your marches on Washington and all that, but my unique brand of activism doesn't end there. I have actually attended one whole Chicago City Council meeting, gone to three—that's right, *three*—political rallies, and have signed *numerous* petitions. Also, I once kissed my girlfriend in public.

Okay, so my political career has been spectacularly lackluster. The truth is, the only kind of lobbying I'm any good at is buying popcorn at the movie theater. And I'm about as politically savvy as Gomer Pyle. I won't go so far as to say I supported Carol Moseley-Braun's bid for senator of Illinois because she's cute as the dickens, but it sure didn't hurt. And I don't want to imply, either, that I'm shallow, but I've never joined Queer Nation because I don't have the proper outfit. Actually, I have huge amounts of respect for all the folks out there on the front lines, pushing the politicos to do the human thing. But personally, I am not cut out for that kind of uphill task. I am much more fit for, say, taking a nap.

Not all choices of dyke style are based on the activities you pursue, of course. Some options have more to do with your essential being—that, and how you dress. For instance, when I first became aware of the butch/femme dichotomy, I was quite confident I was decidedly butch. Having grown up a tomboy with tree climbing—not Barbie—close to my heart and having entirely abandoned dresses for pants sometime in high school, this seemed a perfectly logical assumption to me. It soon became apparent that, to the rest of the lesbian world, I was nothing more than a femme in butch clothing. Respectful of my self-delusion, though, a toothpick-wielding older gal once offered to give me butch lessons—which consisted of instruction on which belt loop to hang my keys from and how to walk like a butch. There may have been more forthcoming in the butch curriculum, but I failed the first part of the course by never demonstrating an aptitude for an authoritative swagger and so we never went on.

Forced to choose between butch and femme, I chose neither—and suffered a severe identity crisis until the nineties brought us crunchy dykes and lipstick lesbians. With my yogurt-eating, lentil-cooking, Birkenstock-wearing, recycling ways, I was a natural for the crunchy dyke. In fact, I have secretly suspected I was the prototype for this class of dyke, which is purportedly named for its love of granola and such. But doubt has started to creep in. I am confronted with philosophical questions like: Can I admit to loving fried foods, Hostess Suzy Q's, and ZZ Top and still be considered a crunchy dyke? Do the tenets of crunchy dykedom allow for one's hair to be artificially curled? And how do I reconcile my techno-culture lifestyle with my crunchy inner being?

What it comes down to is this: I think it is time to admit I *have* no niche in the lesbian community. I am Every Dyke: I'm a little bit crunchy *and* a little bit jock and femme. Oh, how Donny and Marie! In a given burst of lesbians, for instance, I will be the one wearing Birkenstocks, GAP cotton shorts, an International Theatre Festival t-shirt from when Marga Gomez was in town, my baseball cap with a long curly ponytail sticking out the back, a volume of poems in one hand and my girlfriend's hand in the other. Can you pick me out?

Dressing Up Like A Dyke?

As Kermit the frog says, "It's not easy being green." Or being a lesbian, for that matter. Witness: even after you have decided you *are* a lesbian, and even after you have made progress in determining what *brand* of lesbian you are, there is still the requisite fashion statement to formulate. In all honesty, it doesn't pay to sweat this part *too* much. I mean, it's not like they're going to call a press conference or anything to hear how you've decided to present yourself in the lesbian community. Nevertheless, whatever you wear, other lesbians *will* try to interpret your motivations, so this complex topic probably at least bears being thought about.

Not like in the old days, when life was simpler. Back then, the standard fashion statement used to be "no comment," by which we knew that what the lesbian making the statement actually meant, via her pregrunge

grunge, was, "Shove it, you sexist patriarchal pig!" Or words to that effect.

However, unless you have:

a) just stepped out of some antiquated closet;

b) had your head buried in a book, the sand, or some other comparable place; or

c) been living in a suburb of Milwaukee,

you have no doubt noticed lesbian fashion has been changing over the years. A lot. It used to be that the toughest decision I had to make about clothing was which slogan to wear. Now, getting dressed for an outing is much more complex—especially for someone like me who is fond of saying, "Life is a costume party and I like to come appropriately dressed" and means it.

Still, the loosening of the lesbian "fashion" code has opened up whole new worlds to me. Part of this excitement about clothing is a latent childhood kind of thing, dressing up and all—something I skipped right over in my effort to master the pogo stick—a skill that has come in handy in adult life time and again. Another part of my exuberance, certainly, is that some time in my late twenties I discovered that, with the right choice of apparel, I could at least not *look* like a nerd. This was a dramatic breakthrough for someone like me, whose mother had encouraged her to wear makeup so she would look less "nunlike."

This nunlike tendency on my part made me a shoo-in during those Catholic-girls-school days of lesbian dress, the days of the plaid flannel uniform. But as the lesbian community matured and shucked off those old uniforms, it became a little less clear what was replacing them. I, at any rate, went on shopping sprees that defied any sense of conformity. But the new uniform has gradually emerged.

Or rather uniforms. Because one's choice of outfits depends on a range of factors: age, major affiliation within the community, occupation, and so on. Even with this in mind, it's possible for the queer gal of today to branch out from any of these choices to make her own unique fashion statement without raising the hackles of the collective feminist conscience of the community. Bearing this in mind, it might be useful to have a guide to uniforms in the lesbian community, whether you are an avid dyker and use it for identifying dyke types—"Oh look, honey, there's a rare red-crested hairy corporate dyke"—or whether you use it to define where your own affinities lie. Remember, though, dyke style is a much more slippery beast than it used to be and is subject to change without notice.

Dyke Uniforms, circa 1994

The hip young lesbian. Workboots make a comeback. Not paired, however, with jeans or cords as with the seventies-generation dyke but, rather, with shorts and patterned hose or with a simple frock. Hair tends to be either mostly not there and/or in primary colors. Accessories are de rigueur. Wherever a hunk of metal can adorn the human body it does: lip, nose, eyebrow, nipple, navel, labia, tongue. I often wonder how these gals get through the metal detector at the airport. "Lipstick lesbians" are the femmy end of this continuum.

The leather chick. The watchword here is, the more leather the better: leather pants or chaps, leather vest—with or without a Dago-t—studded wrist bands and dog collar, leather motorcycle boots, motorcycle jacket with as many metal buckles and zippers as can be added and still have room for that butch black leather. A good outfit if you like your lesbians moist. Doesn't all that leather chafe, though? And I haven't even mentioned the leather underwear. . . . Accessories tend to be of the permanent variety: tattoos of bald eagles, labyrises, the Harley Davidson logo—although bandannas prove to be quite the versatile adornment, from headbands to tail feathers.

Queer Nation/ACT UP babe. Doc Martens boots, black leather jacket plastered with political stickers, and power lunch or Silence = Death t-shirt.

Crunchy dyke. Birkenstocks and a Meat Is Murder t-shirt. Accessories range from crystals and giant labyrises to pink triangles.

Brand X lesbian. Seriously into GAP wear and other relatively bland/comfortable clothing. Sensible shoes are the order of the day: Doc Martens, Teva sandals, Birkenstocks, flip-flops, or sneakers—practicality is the key. Accessories are minimal, but may include a tasteful pink triangle or a Names Project button. Wears a fanny pack at all times. If she has a tattoo, it is most likely a tiny unicorn, butterfly, or rose and is on the shoulder or ankle.

The suburban dyke. Big hair, a carefully creased ensemble from Bloomingdale's or Lord and Taylor, flats. Hey wait a minute—I think I just described my girlfriend's mom!

Your basic jock. GAP-type wear, all the way, except for the shoes, which are seriously athletic, featuring an assortment of Velcro straps, breathing fabrics, eyelets, arch supports, and layered soles, the functions of which I am only vaguely aware. A baseball cap is a must. Frequently seen toting a gym bag. Tattoos are a possibility but not really necessary as her body is likely to be decorated at most times with an assortment of bruises, cuts, raspberries, and scars, which she wears like badges of honor.

The corporate dyke. Khaki or navy suit, gym shoes over anklets and nylons, a strategically placed ruffle on the blouse for that hint o' femininity, and an Eddie Bauer "briefcase." Hair is severely coiffeured. Wears one earring in each ear. Oops—just described my girlfriend's mother again.

The budding baby dyke. Just beginning to experiment with these different styles: Birkenstocks and a pierced lip, an I Can't Even Think Straight t-shirt and GAP shorts, stickers and buttons on her backpack.

The old guard. Still wearing those blue jeans and Holly Near t-shirts.

How does a girl today choose? Personally, I like to mix and match, although I have to admit I'm a little low on leather wear and I've managed to keep the number of holes in my body fairly close to the number I was born with. But if I had to characterize myself, until recently, I'd have said I fell into the Brand X category. Until recently, I say, because lately, something strange has been happening to me.

I am concerned, to be specific, that I might have taken an overdose of Fem Iron—except for the minor detail that I've never taken the stuff. The cause of this irrational concern is that, in the last year or two, I seem to be getting in touch with my feminine side. I haven't gone totally berserk, mind you—I mean, you'd never mistake me for a drag queen or Tammy Wynette or anything—but little by little, femmy touches have been creeping into my life. I have even found myself humming (to the tune of that Diana Ross hit a decade back) "I'm Femming Up."

It all started innocently enough, as these things usually do. I wanted to get a perm so I wouldn't have to mess around with my hair so much. And because I didn't want to be dropping eighty or a hundred dollars every month or two, I decided to grow my hair long so the perm wouldn't be getting cut off all the time. I swear that was all I intended! And, I don't mean to sound defensive, but even though my hair is now long and voluptuous and curly, it's still very utilitarian. Really. There's absolutely no styling involved. Of course, if I were to tell the truth, which I seem to do compulsively (should I be in therapy for that?) the no-styling thing is less a political statement of any sort than a result of my own hair-styling ineptitude. When I use a blow drier, for instance, I only succeed in making my hair look wind blown, not neat.

Anyway, that's the way it started, with the long hair. The next thing I knew, I found myself thinking I might like to buy a dress—something I'd never before willingly done. In fact, the last time I purchased a skirt or dress of any kind was in the early eighties when I was a prisoner of corporate life and, as part of my punishment, I was made to wear uncomfortable clothing. Although, now that I think about it, I did grow frighteningly fond of that pink skirt with the six-inch slit up the left side. . . . Help! I'm having an Evan Picone flashback. No, no—it's okay. I'm all right now. . . I think—except for this dress-buying obsession, which I valiantly fought for almost a year before succumbing. Again, in my defense, it's not one of those frilly numbers that shows lots of cleavage—like I have any to show anyway—but a no-nonsense seersucker number with tiny blue and white checks, one of those jumper things. Actually, more than one person has commented on my resemblance, when so clothed, to Dorothy of *Wizard of Oz* fame—which is not *exactly* the look I was going for. I know I'm not really equipped to pull off the whole Madonna gestalt (I'm not even really sure what a bustier is), but I *was* hoping for something a little sexier than the farm girl image. Of course, the turquoise tights I bought to go with the ensemble don't help much: from the waist down I look like a smurf. At any rate, the dress is comfortable and my girlfriend thinks I look cute in it, so that's all that really matters, or so I tell myself. But still: it's a dress, no matter how many disclaimers I may issue. . . .

There are other signs, too, that somewhere deep inside me there's a femme trying to come out. For example, I recently had my office at home painted. I agonized for weeks over what color it should be. A warm rust color, I thought at first. Or maybe a restful shade of blue. Or a light gray-green. And what did I end up with? Dusty rose—or in layperson's terms: pink. To be honest, I have never really thought of myself as a pink person—it's such a wussy color. And yet, after having just confessed my wall-color choice and my affection for that pink skirt, I find I am being forced to come to grips with the fact that I have apparently been harboring a secret love, all these years, for that color so stereotypically associated with girls. But hey, maybe it's time to reclaim the color pink so butches and feminists everywhere can proudly display their pink triangles on a stunning field of matching pink!

But there's one more thing I should mention, I suppose: I pluck my eyebrows. This is not, however, a particularly new thing with me (which makes it oh-so-much better, I know). But it's not even that my eyebrows are so thick and bushy that, *sans* plucking, people would confuse me with Groucho Marx or Einstein—despite my charming little hint of mustache. On the contrary, my eyebrows, in their natural state, are scattered lightly and randomly around the over-the-eye area like iron filings in one of those Wooly Willie kids' things where you create facial-hair fashion statements with a magnet. Whoever did me didn't do such a good job; I'm just trying to tidy up a little.

Fortunately, I am secure enough in my inner butchness not to feel threatened by these outward displays of femininity. Maybe it's just a phase. Maybe I'll grow out of it—I used to like the musical stylings of David Gates and Bread and I grew out of that! Or maybe it's just one aspect of my multifaceted and enigmatic personality. Chicago writer Kathie Bergquist has "accused" me of "messing with her mind"—of being neither butch nor femme. And in a way, I guess she's right: I am not, as a rule, a gal who is given to extremes, except for that time when I went out shopping for a baseball cap, couldn't find one in my size, and so came home with a VCR instead. At any rate, I am not about to give up my extensive collection of t-shirts, shorts, and sports equipment for an assortment of color-coordinated pumps, support-top taupe panty hose, and lipsticks with oh-so-subtle names like Lusty Rose, Passion Pink, and Kiss Me Carnation. Still, I suspect there's room in my closet for another delightful little frock or two. . . .

But as long as I'm discussing fashion, let me ask you this: When did *Hats* become such a lesbian thing? I pay pretty close attention to lesbians—How come I hadn't noticed Hats had become such a *thing*?

This, at any rate, is what I was thinking while looking at the throngs of dykes stuffing the aisles of the 1991 Mid-Winter Crafts Festival at Mountain Moving Coffeehouse in Chicago—"the lesbian mall," as one of our local celebs dubbed it. I was sitting behind a *card* table hawking my wares, right next to, appropriately enough, considering my table, the Dyke Deck women with their lesbian playing cards.

At my own little card table, I was trying to look alluring or something when I was struck by the number of women wearing interesting and exotic hats—a number that increased over the course of the day owing, I later learned, to the two or three craftswomen vending their cap creations. But selling doesn't necessarily lead to buying, as I can tell you from my own experience—why the sudden fedora frenzy? It wasn't even cold outside. . . .

When I contemplated this phenomenon, I found myself thinking: historically, lesbians (and I generalize here, I know) have tended to sport headgear primarily for practical reasons, wearing something with earflaps or visors, as the demands of the season advised.

Exceptions to this were generally found among African-American lesbians, on whom I had noted some magnificent millinery—for no other reason, apparently, than that they (the hats *and* the women) looked good. But I had always assumed it was more of an African-American thing than a lesbian thing. I see now I must have been wrong or that, at least, we have our African-American sisters to thank for introducing us to this fashion option.

Having plenty of time to mull this over between sales, I was just priding myself on having neatly dissected this pithy conundrum when visions of headwear past came bubbling slowly into my brain. Picture this: a woman with a shag haircut, wearing a black three-piece suit with flared (perhaps bell-bottom) pants and gold piping on the vest, carrying a drink tray to the tune of "I Need a Man." Whose face is it, under that black felt hat? Gasp! It's mine.

It all came back to me then, how I, a lowly nerd from Milwaukee, had emulated the fashion sense of my heart-throb-from-afar, that immigrant from Brooklyn to the Midwest, the first lesbian my little baby dyke heart ever knowingly beat for. I, who had never worn hats, even in the dead of winter or the blinding sun of summer, had shopped for ostentatious felt hats.

Of course it's easy to look back at the seventies now, from the vantage point of the nineties, and scoff at the ridiculousness of me in such an ensemble, but back then . . . I looked ridiculous. Not the least because I could never find hats to fit. I have a rather diminutive cranium and am affectionately, I like to think, known as Zippy the Pinhead. You can imagine how sexy I must have looked, with that hat perched right there on my ears, threatening to fall down over my eyes the minute I removed my glasses.

But even in those now dark disco days, my Italian stallionette shero and I notwithstanding, it tended to be the gay men and not the lesbians who were flamboyant; I don't recall hats being a big thing with us lezzies even then. And when disco died, so did my hat-wearing days—so much so, in fact, that my girlfriend had to badger me for years before I was willing to buy some sort of head covering for the bitter winter months in Chicago.

I am not fundamentally a hat person. But I don't know. Somehow, as dykes with hats multiplied before my eyes like something out of a children's story, I became enchanted with the notion of owning one of those hats. When my girlfriend unwittingly agreed to take over the so-called sales table for me, I purposefully made my way around the room looking for the source of hats.

Once the source was found, I made five or six trips back with my lover and various unsuspecting friends, watching their faces to see how I looked with one of these funky fezzes adorning my noggin, trying to decide if I really had the chutzpah to wear one. Between forays to the chapeau table, I philosophized with the Dyke Deck women on the wearing of hats, pondering such issues as the hat-wearing persona: How is it made? And could I get it? After much deliberation of this sort, I bought A Hat.

I am sure that in describing it, I won't do it justice, but I'll give it a try anyway. It's a cotton patchwork kind of thing, maybe like a skullcap with a thyroid condition or a pillbox hat that hugs the head. It's bright and winsome and whimsical. And, most important, I feel great wearing it. It is not the perfect cap, though, as far as my lover is concerned: it doesn't cover my ears. But it may perform other valuable functions.

For instance: I had been commenting to a friend that lately, when I do poetry readings, I feel like I'm not weird enough to be a poet, that I'm too *normal* looking. After the Mini-Fest, my new hat resting jauntily on my head, my friend assured me: "If you wear that hat to poetry readings, no one will mess with you." In the words of Richard Pryor: I'm bad. I'm bad. Uh huh. I just hope this cap doesn't end up a museum piece like the black felt number. *Lesbianus skullcapus,* circa 1991.

Okay, I admit it: beneath this glib veneer of rationality and wit lies a simpering mass of fear: first dresses, then this outré hat business—*what's next?* Will the femme within execute a hostile takeover, forcing me to sneak Avon catalogs and Lady Schick razors into the house? Or will whichever alien took over my body force me to go off in some other perverse direction? Like, will I suddenly wake up some morning with an overpowering urge to listen to Buck Owens music and put on clothes involving large amounts of fringe and tooled leather? Or will I feel compelled to cut off all my hair except for a long swatch on top, wear bed sheets, and hang out at airports? The possibilities are overwhelming.

But if Sigourney Weaver can kick ass with her alien, I'm sure I can hold my own with whatever nellie little extraterrestrial is making me wear "women's" clothing! That's the beauty of being of the female persuasion: other than jock straps or jockey shorts, pretty much *everything* is women's clothing.

Okay, everybody now: "When I have a brand new hairdo, and my eyelashes all in curls, I float as the clouds in air do—*I enjoy being a girl.*"

A Bevy Of Lezzies

Lesbians by ones or by twos, unless engaging in daring PDAs (public displays of affection—which are, as you know, especially daring if performed by only one lesbian), have a tendency to pretty much blend in with the masses. Hence this cloak of invisibility thing we've been trying to divest ourselves of for some time now. It's like we've all been hanging with Wonder Woman in that invisible plane of hers, and now that we're deplaning in Northampton, Mass., everyone else is wondering how the heck we got here and, more important, who cleared us for landing.

Anyway, the point is that, singly, we're not that distinguishable from regular folk: if you feed us organic produce, do we not eat? But lesbians in groups are a horse of a different culture. What other group, historically, has paid such close scrutiny to the political implications of whether its legs were hairy or shorn? What other community has been so sensitive to every shade of "ism" that they have essentially appropriated the concept of "processing"? Why, it could only be the lesbians, of course.

What I'm telling you is that lesbians are a very organized people. Not that we are necessarily good at organizing the elements of our *private* lives—witness the "basket of shame" in my office, where I dump all artifacts of the written word I feel I should save but don't know where the heck to file. We do, however, excel at organizing *people*. Many of us, I think, harbor a secret yearning to be girl scout leaders. Or commandants. Every time you turn around, lesbians are orchestrating large unwieldy things. If it's not a festival, it's a march on the nation's capital. Or a presidential cabinet department. Or a softball league.

If you think that, in terms of scope, softball doesn't fit in with the other things on the list, you don't know *lesbian* softball, sister. First off, lesbian softball isn't just a few gals gathering together in one or two cities for a little game of pick-up softball. It is women in cities, towns, and rural areas all across the country and into Canada playing *organized* softball. I don't mean to imply that there's, like, a dyke softball czarina or anything, sitting on a throne in the royal dugout, overseeing her softball subjects across the land, establishing diplomatic relations with lesbian rugby teams, and spitting royal chewing tobacco on the royal floor. But numerous cities have actual lesbian leagues, complete with playoffs, tournaments, spectators, and beer coolers.

It is no small thing to keep a league like that going. For example, you have to find a field or fields where if the lesbians play clearly exceptional ball the nearby men's teams don't feel a need to reaffirm their masculinity in another way altogether—like punching out a few dykes. You also need a playing field with restrooms nearby because women tend to be rather partial to indoor plumbing—as opposed to men who are much more in touch with their *natural* side. Once the field is found, you must work out the time table—being careful not to schedule games on the major holidays, like the 4th of July, Pride Day, and the Michigan Womyn's Music Festival. (Father's Day, however, is generally not considered sacrosanct.)

What it is that makes lesbian softball something of a miracle, though, is that, often, *the teams are entirely made up of lesbians.* This is only miraculous when you consider that it is no simple matter to keep up team spirit—or keep up a team period—when *X* refuses to catch for *Y* and won't follow *Z* in the batting line-up because *Y* just dumped *X* and has shamelessly taken up with *Z*. Furthermore, these patterns can shift several times during the course of one season, or, in really advanced cases, during one game. And given that whole teams sometimes have the same haircut, it can get very confusing. Even more amazing, though, is how many teams actually function well, composed, as they are, of complicated webs of lovers and ex-lovers, all mingling together on the ball field like one big happy incestuous family. I suspect this is a situation that comes up very seldom in the majors. Personally, I think it is the ex-lover factor that in large part accounts for the ban on metal cleats in the league I played in. Of course, there are still all those bats lying around. . . .

In contrast, teams not currently engaged in one furious round after another of musical lovers can be like a big old extended family—and just as dysfunctional too. Sometimes, when Bitsy, who plays first, is leering at some gal on the other team and making crude comments, and Letitia, at short, is splattering chewing tobacco on your brand new cleats and Butch, the pitcher, is whining about her broken nail, you find yourself thinking, "I can't believe I'm *related* to these people!" And then you realize you're not—which is a good thing when you consider how prone lesbians are to sleep with other members of the team.

Still, you might as well be related to your teammates, around and among whom you chart the course of your life each season. Actually, you probably see them way more often than you do the people with whom you share identical overbites and cowlicks. Not only are there the games, but there are also the practices, the after-game barbecues, the birthday parties, the outings to movies and concerts, and the small group sessions in which you philanthropically set out to determine exactly what are the problems of everyone else on the team. Why, by the end of the season, team members can become so comfortable with one another that they can communicate with nothing more than a curled lip or a turned back.

What is truly family-like about these teams, though, is that, in spite of all the tensions that can arise during the course of a season and in spite of the many declarations of intentions not to play again the following year, come sign-up time, virtually the whole gang is right there again, just like always. Teams have been known to stay together for years and years, although as attrition takes its toll, the entire character of the team may change and the name may change several times as part of the witness relocation program.

The team I started playing on nearly a decade ago, for example, was a laid-back recreational sort of team, with which I fit in very nicely due to my ability to bobble a ball for several minutes in the field before the runner could confidently be called safe or out. In this way, I was able, single-handedly, to increase the suspense level of the game. As the years went by and departing players were gradually replaced, I somehow found myself on a team that shouted encouragement to one another by saying things like "C'mon: you've got ducks on the pond" and "Turn two!" and who could, in fact, "turn two" in the time it normally took me simply to get the ball under control. My patented suspense-raising method was now unappreciated, so I took my talent elsewhere. On my new team, the phrase "ducks on the pond," which I brought with me, transmogrified into "There's bread in the oven" and "There are cars in the garage," while "Turn two" was discarded altogether as being more liable, among the likes of us, to refer to ankles than to plays. My old teammates, like the spouses of one's divorced siblings, have totally disappeared from my life.

Scads more could be said about softball, of course. In fact, I could write a book about it. (Oh wait a minute—I already did.) Anyway, what I'm getting at is that lesbians have taken a sport loved by many and transformed it not only into something with very much their own flavor but also into the one constant and universally common characteristic of lesbian populations nationwide: bars and bookstores and social groups come and go, but there will always be softball. For a community that can't even agree on what we should be called, that's really something. Should we be called gay? Or dykes? Or lesbians? Or womyn-loving womyn? Personally, I prefer to be called She Who Walks in Cleated Splendor. The one thing we do agree on, as I say, is softball. As evidence of the universality of softball's draw, I offer my friend Kathie Bergquist and her team the Tarts, a self-described group of girlie girls who, until the summer of 1994, had never played softball and whose uniforms consisted of cropped t-shirts and lipstick. (I am assuming they wore some sort of apparel on the lower portion of their torsos as well, although this was not specifically mentioned.) This example alone, my friends, gives you some idea of what kind of mysterious power softball has over the lesbian population.

While softball may be the oldest and most ubiquitous organizing factor in the lesbian community, it is certainly no longer the only one. If you're missing the girl scouts, for instance, yet want something with a little more edge to it, many cities have some sort of branch of the Lesbian Avengers. The Avengers perform all sorts of cool direct action, like organizing marches to improve lesbian visibility and leafletting various types of gatherings with information on lesbian civil rights. I would love to have seen it when, on Valentine's Day in 1994, they built a statue of Alice B. Toklas next to the one of Gertrude Stein in Central Park in New York and then lectured the crowd about lesbian visibility. What I want to know is, what the heck did they build the statue with—a large molded brownie? I am thinking of joining, but only if I get to wear a mask and a cape.

By far the most fabulous organization in the lesbian community, though, is the music festival. A lesbian—a.k.a. "women's"—music festival is like a landlocked version of what we like to think of as the *true* island of Lesbos: nothing but dykes as far as the eye can see. Well, plus a few token straight women; to the best of my knowledge, no one checks your credentials at the gate. In any case, the festivals are the one place where lesbians are in the distinct majority and can live without fear of anything worse than a bad sunburn, an excruciating run-in with an ex-lover, or a hotly raging political debate.

It used to be that when it came to festival going, you pretty much had two choices: Michigan and the National. Now, I don't even know how many festivals there are. Having been only to the aforementioned two, I can't really speak to what the other festivals are like. Nevertheless, this doesn't stop me from saying that, in my mind, I suspect the Michigan Womyn's Music Festival will always reign supreme. With so many options—you've got your southern, west coast, and east coast festivals, just to name a few—why, you might reasonably ask, would I make this outrageous claim?

It all centers on the fact that, yes, I am a camping snob. I have tried to work through these nonfeminist feelings I have about the naturophobic. But in spite of my best efforts, I am still occasionally haunted by renegade feelings of superiority when I meet those who are challenged by setting up a tent; by cold, infrequent showers; by food prepared to less than gourmet standards; and by not having access to blow driers for today's complex hairstyles. I cannot conquer my pride at being a "rough-and-tumble kind of gal," as my grandmother would describe me. The pleasure I take in camping is no doubt a manifestation of my butch side.

At any rate, given these campist tendencies on my part, you can well imagine my disgust at hearing that at some of these other "outdoor" women's music festivals they actually feature such wimpy things as *cabins, beds,* and *warm showers.* Where is it written, you may be asking, that women's music festivals must feature camping? Like anyone under the influence of an "ism," I am not completely rational on this matter. I don't deny there should be space in the world of women's festivals for those who can't—either physically or emotionally—deal with the ruggedness of camping, but that long-standing tradition at Michigan has forever linked "camping" and "festival" for me: there is now a certain mystique, a certain nostalgia, surrounding this combination. Then, too, at the risk of sounding too darn spiritual, there is just something primal about the ancient rhythms of the music vibrating through the land and through yourself as you are there, one with nature. It's beautiful, man.

But to return to the subject of my pride: as part of my penance for not conquering this sinful emotion, I have decided to share with the festi virgins among you the various bits of knowledge I have gained over the years as a Michigan festival devotee. The first thing is, if you're not a compulsive list maker, find a lover or friend who is. Braving the wilds requires you to pack things you don't ordinarily need when vacationing at the Hawaii Hilton—like toilet paper, a flashlight, long johns, and silverware, to name but a few—and trying to keep track of the odd item here or there is next to impossible without a running list. My lover Kathy teases me about being anal-retentive regarding my list-making penchant because I jotted down ninety items in the first draft of our Michigan list one year. I knew, however, that when she got that life-threatening hangnail and I was there to rescue her with my trusty nail clippers she could not help but be grateful.

After glomming onto a list maker, but before you attempt to compose said list, you need to weigh the hassle of lugging things back and forth between car and campsite versus your comfort while you are there. This is an equation that can usually only be balanced over time. One woman I know hates the lugging part so much that she brings as few things as possible. Other women are so committed to comfort that they are willing to sacrifice both their backs and any semblance of being surrounded by nature, bringing with them giant coolers of assorted beverages and meats, grills, battery-operated TVs, small stereo systems, picnic tables and chairs, portable showers—in short, all the comforts of home. There's something to be said for this level of comfort and how it can enhance the overall pleasure of your stay, but some of us would get so grumpy having to haul all of that stuff that we would never really ungrump enough to enjoy our time there. Relationships, I'm telling you, have been made and broken over the setting up of camp. . . .

Once you've determined how many parts pack horse you are versus how many parts slave to comfort, you can begin constructing the list itself. There are five highly technical categories of list items, each with its own idiosyncrasies: grooming and health care; clothing; camping equipment; food; and, most technical of all, other stuff. In list making, I leave nothing to either chance or memory—which in my case are synonymous. I write everything down. Kathy finds it hard to believe I could actually forget to bring underwear and that I feel it's necessary to write myself a reminder, but in my frenzy to make sure I've packed the wineskin and the hair goop, anything's possible.

Now. To the specifics. The grooming and health care category is pretty straightforward: shampoo, soap, sun screen, aloe gel, Garfield band-aids. Clothing, however, is somewhat deceptive—at least for camping at Michigan. Although you will be there for less than a week, it is wise to pack for all four seasons: rain gear for spring rains; shorts and flip-flops for hot summer days; jeans and a jacket for autumnal evenings under the stars; and long underwear for what can feel like wintry sleeping conditions. The last time I gave this advice, however, the temperature never dipped below about 79°F; women were cussing me out for causing them to give up valuable tank top space in their back packs for long underwear. The moral of that story is, whatever clothes you pack for Michigan will be wrong. Fortunately, you can buy any sort of bodily adornment you might need in the crafts area, including the never-out-of-season nipple ring.

Getting back to the list, camping gear is not as simple a list as it sounds either. Not only is it important to remember the tent stakes, but you should have something to pound them in with too. As for food, for those who are allergic to healthy eating, this is a critical portion of your Michigan list. I myself have no objections to the vegetarian fare served there, but it does tend to be underspiced so I usually bring at least salt and pepper with me. Finally, there's the category of "other stuff," which encompasses anything that doesn't fit elsewhere on the list but generally could be subtitled, for my purposes, "entertainment": toys, games, something to read—as if the festival doesn't provide stimulation enough on its own.

Now you just have to figure out how to get all this junk—and your lover—into the car. Of course, if the former is not executed carefully, you may not have to worry about the latter being in the car after all. It's all part of the Michigan experience.

However, if you are one of the eight lesbians in your town who won't be going to Michigan in a given year or if you're a man and you've always wondered what the Michigan festival gestalt is all about, cheer up: there *is* something you can do. All you have to do is follow these simple steps to create your own Michigan Womyn's Music Festival experience.

1. Find a road with a LOT of potholes (almost any street in Chicago), and drive over and over it, imagining that the phone poles along the sidewalks are really trees and that the blue cloud of smoke around you is the dust of a dirt road instead of the environmental disaster of a car choking along in front of you. While you drive, have on a tape of the Parachute Club or Holly Near and an idiotic grin of happiness and say things like, "We're almost there!" and, "Won't be long now!"

2. When you return home from this drive, put together a complicated piece of equipment in the dark with nothing but a flashlight to illuminate the tricky parts. Maybe, for good measure, have a little argument with your lover about which thingumabob gets inserted where.

3. Give the different rooms in your house names, like Lunatic Fringe, Neptune Nerds, and Spinster Acres. Assign different rules of behavior to each room and sleep in the one that best suits your mood.

4. Spend the next three or four days walking around your house with nothing on but Birkenstocks.

5. Sleep on the floor. Or, for a more authentic effect, try scattering several pretzel sticks and garbanzo beans (uncooked) under your sleeping bag or blanket. Release a few mosquitoes into the room, and cuddle up to your honey.

6. The next morning, scatter gravel on the floor of your shower and turn on the spigot for cold full blast, seasoning it with just a hint of warm. Invite several women from the community, whether you know them or not, to come watch.

7. Sit out in the sun way too long and crisp up those tender parts. Don't drink any water until you feel as if you could pass out.

8. Walk twice around the perimeter of your house, very slowly, before getting food, then sit down on your lawn, with the sprinkler on, to eat. If you are the sort of person who is always prepared, it's okay to hold a rain poncho, tentlike, over your head and your plate while you attempt to dine.

9. Go into your house, turn out all of the lights, crank up the air conditioning to "freeze," take off most or all of your clothes, and put a damp blanket on the floor. Then, put on a tape of Cris Williamson and relax. For an even more realistic effect, you could also turn on a sitcom so all the talking and laughing make it hard to really hear the music.

10. Don't look at a newspaper or listen to any news for several days running so you have no idea what's going on in the world outside.

11. Start a rumor. And then tell yourself it's not true.

12. You could try not flushing the toilet for three or four days, but the neighbors would probably complain. When they do, and the Board of Health comes to investigate, holler, "Men on the Land!" as you open the door—unless, of course, the bureaucrat in question is a woman. In which case, by all means: invite her in.

13. Invite all of your ex-lovers over and glare at them as you pass from room to room.

14. Argue with yourself about the political correctness of every possible issue.

But before you run around and start making all sorts of modifications to your living quarters—like hauling in a truckload of gravel for the shower and shutting off the hot water—I should tell you that, even though you might be able to re-create the physical sensations of the Michigan experience, there's just no other way to capture the thrill of being surrounded by a burst of lesbians and all the many facets of our culture without actually going *to* the festival. It's like lesbian concentrate: nutritious and delicious. Just add yourself and stir.

Dates, Nuts, And Serial TV

All I know is, I'm glad I'm not dating anymore.

If the truth be told, like most lesbians I know, I never quite got the hang of it. And having always heard, "If you can't do something right, don't do it at all," most of us skip right over that awkward dating stage and just move in together. Well, it solves the messy problem of what to wear on a date—and creates about a dozen others. Furthermore, unless your new honey is named Attila, your friends are no help here either: after you've dated someone two or three times, you can go nowhere alone without inquiring minds wanting to know where your other half is—as if you had recently become an amoeba and had carelessly misplaced the result of your mitotic effort. Still, you would think those other problems would be enough to dissuade us from such rash moves, but apparently our ineptitude at dating is greater than our fear of jumping head first into the untested water.

Just why is that? Why can't lesbians—people who are smart enough to deconstruct language and who are capable enough to turn a few acres of forest into a city every summer (I refer of course to *the holy* city: the Michigan Womyn's Music Festival)—why don't we do dating very well? Well, in view of the fact that no enterprising young sociologist has elected to study this fascinating aspect of human behavior, I'll just go right ahead and make something up. Here's what I think:

First of all, even if you *know* you're a lesbian in high school, the time from which all dating knowledge dates, it's not as though you can exactly play the field: there usually aren't all that many other baby dykes who are precocious enough to be out—unless of course you went to a Catholic girls' high school. I don't know from personal experience, having been raised many shades of Protestant myself, but I've heard that those Catholic girls were having all sorts of religious experiences. It's true what they say: you just can't get a good education in the public schools. . . .

Anyway, even if there were plenty of baby dykes from whom to choose, most schools/parents/teenagers weren't so open-minded that you could hang out with your best gal with the other kids at the malt shop or the big game. Lesbian dating in high school is necessarily an intimate thing. If you can't hold hands with each other in the bleachers like all the other couples, you improvise: move to your girlfriend's bedroom or your parents' basement—all the time with one ear cocked toward the door. And that's how the whole nasty cycle gets started: already, we're skipping stages.

Of course, if you don't know you're a lesbian in high school, you may be dating boys. This, you might think, would give us that precious experience we need. Still, at least for those of us raised in the fifties, sixties, or seventies, it was the boys who were in charge. Which meant that, just because we were dating, didn't mean we knew how to *do* it. The boys did the asking out, the planning of the whens and wheres, and the instigating of any necking that went on. We were part of the plan, not the makers of the plan. We were merely the support staff to upper management, never privy to the top secret information of how not to take things too seriously, of how to get what you could from every situation, then move on. The right training is oh-so-important.

Still, I suppose it's not entirely fair to blame all of our troubles on the public school system and being shut out of the young boys' network. Part of our problem, I suspect, is sheer laziness: it is just plain hard work to date. It is much easier to settle back and start taking each other for granted than to keep racking your brains to come up with ways to meet new people—especially people of the lesbian variety. I mean, what are our options? Softball? After one season, no one on the team is "new" anymore. In fact, of the women who aren't in couples, you will no doubt have been in *relationships* with one or two of them from one season to the next. Consequently, after that first season, softball is pretty much tapped out for its dating potential—unless you move from team to team, a sort of roving designated hitter.

So what's left? The Metropolitan Community Church? I'm guessing it too may have a fairly limited population from which to draw—but perhaps that's just my heathen ignorance. Queer Nation meetings? Sure, why not, if you go in for a younger crowd. Although personally, I would never fit in: I don't even *own* a black leather jacket and combat boots. The bars? That's certainly the usual option. And in my younger years, as I've said, I spent my fair share of time there; these days I just get cranky about all the cigarette smoke and the lack of places to sit. But even when I was frequenting the bars, I was never very good at "doing the bars"—in spite of the coaching I received from my friends. I think that I'm just barfly-impaired. However, I don't want to deny the information I stored away over the years to those who could actually use it. So here, for your perusal, is the collected wisdom of the few, the proud, the brave—the women who know how to "do the bars."

1. Develop a skill. This is probably the most fundamental of all the guidelines. Of course, I don't mean to imply that any skill will do; it has to be one you can easily (and decently!) perform in a bar. It would be a bit awkward, for instance, to cart along a few boards, nails, and tools with you to show off your woodworking skills. The skills most often suggested to me as appropriate and valuable to acquire were shooting pool, dancing, and making small talk. If you're planning on hanging out at a swanky dance bar, shooting pool is probably not your best choice. Personally, I hang out at such bars just so I *won't* have to shoot pool. I always thought I would be pretty adept at billiards, having been good at geometry in high school. But somehow, my ability for determining angles on paper never transferred to felt. Maybe if I had brought my protractor. . . .

Dancing is a good skill, I guess. It accomplishes, at minimum, two things. It gives you at least one sentence to say to someone ("Would you like to dance?") and, if you're a smooth dancer, you can impress the hell out of women. But I dunno, it can also backfire, it seems to me. As an impromptu sort of dancer myself (that is, someone who makes it up as she goes along), I've been intimidated as hell by some of those fancy dancers. Dance with one of them? Are you kidding? And embarrass myself to death?

As for small talk, I don't know what to tell you, except that it's very important—and it's a talent I never acquired. My friend would coach me, saying, "Just talk about something you're interested in." And I would say, "What am I supposed to say—'Hi. Do you like the Indigo Girls?'" I just don't have a "feel" for it, I guess. I have a tendency to want to leap past the topics of weather, politics, observations about the bar's atmosphere, or *whatever* it is people talk about when they're making small talk. I want to get right into important things like: Where do you stand on monogamy versus nonmonogamy? Are you allergic to cats? How do you feel about S/M? What's your philosophy of life?—clearly not material for easing into a conversation at a bar.

2. Watch your language. Body language, that is. My friends were always yelling at me about standing around with my arms folded over my chest—bad body language. But I didn't mean to be saying "Stay away"—I just wanted a place to put my arms! Pants pockets can help with that, I guess. Then you can hook your thumbs into your pockets, lean casually against the wall, maybe one shoulder a little higher than the other one . . . well, anyway, you get the picture.

3. Don't travel in a pack. While there's a real temptation to take friends with you when you go so you won't be alone and bummed (instead, you can be bummed out in the company of people you know), it cuts you off from a lot of casual contacts. For one thing, the way we hug and kiss our friends, it can be hard for a stranger to figure out who is just a friend and who is a lover. Actually, sometimes it can be hard for people who *know* us to figure that out! And most dykes are wary of hitting on someone else's lover—especially in front of that lover. For another thing, most of us get terribly embarrassed about being rejected. And if there is the risk of displaying that embarrassment to a whole burst of lesbians, most dykes will decide to forgo the risk.

4. Carry a cigarette lighter. That way, you can run around offering to light women's cigarettes for them. I've never tried this one myself, but I imagine if you want to meet someone who smokes, it's the perfect opener. I suspect it works best if you wait to make your offer until you actually *see* the woman with a cigarette.

5. Offer to buy a drink. This can work under the right circumstances, but many women will be cautious about such an offer, recalling, perhaps, that time-honored cliché, "There's no such thing as a free lunch."

6. Be careful about "packaging." The way a person dresses says a lot about them. Though it's true you can't judge a book by its cover (oops—must have accidentally left the cliché bin open), unless you're an opposites-attract-kinda-gal, if you dress preppy, you're probably not going to hit it off real well with someone dressed in a studded leather jacket, torn jeans, and chartreuse hair. So while you may be tempted to dress in a way that will make you more noticeable, you need to be aware of what kind of messages are being sent by those painted-on jeans or that red bandanna in your back left pocket.

7. Wear comfortable shoes. If you're going to stand

around all night, making small talk, shooting pool, or dancing, you might as well be comfortable. Besides, shoes that pinch your feet probably aren't going to do a whole lot for the expression on your face.

But okay, so let's say you're not the lazy type or you are, but you have natural bar-fly talents and so have managed to meet someone anyway—that still doesn't solve the essential problem of actually dating. That's the missing step here: *(1)* you meet someone, *(3)* you're dynamo-ing your names together on the mailbox. What happened to *(2)*? It all goes back, I maintain, to that lack of early experience.

Nevertheless, it's not like we didn't all have TVs or anything: we were familiar with the concept of dating, of how it worked, and what it was supposed to accomplish. We've all seen "Love American Style," "The Dating Game," and "The Love Connection," for heaven's sake! Of course, that should have been our first clue this dating stuff was not as easy as one might think. If it were easy, would people willingly subject themselves to the humiliation of being on "The Dating Game"? Of having Jim Lang, the host, smirk and leer at them? I have been thinking maybe it's time we, in the lesbian community, admitted we could use our own version of "The Dating Game."

The first thing we need to do is find a host, by which, of course, I mean a lesbian, even though I say "host," the masculine form of the word that means "to smile a lot inanely and make stupid jokes with sexual innuendos." I choose this word form not out of any veiled reference to a butch/femme dichotomy or anything nearly so political but because "hostess" always makes me think of a sponge-like black cupcake oozing unidentifiable sweet stuff.

Apparently, I am not the only one to make this sort of unfortunate connection because nary a game show in TV history (there are a scant one or two exceptions) has been hosted by a woman—and the cupcake thing is the only possible reason for it, I'm sure. . . .

No matter: lesbians are used to breaking new ground, to going where no man has gone before—only in this case, it would be going where no woman has gone before. That's okay: we've done that too. In any case, we need a host who is charming, witty, quick on her feet—lesbian feminist comedian Kate Clinton comes to mind. But then again, when doesn't she? On further reflection, Kate might not be a good choice: everyone would want to date her rather than the other contestants—a problem I somehow can't imagine Jim Lang ever had. (Straight friends assure me this is not just a lesbian bias.) What we need then, is someone who can deal with that transference thing, someone like a therapist who has to deal with that sort of thing all the time—someone like JoAnn Loulan, the Dr. Ruth of lesbians. Why not? She has the same appealing qualities that Kate has *plus* she can do couples counseling after the contestants have their first date!

Now, let's see—what else? Well, we would have to plan where the dates would be. There were always several dates to nearby, ordinary kinds of places and then one or two to exciting, exotic locales. So, we could do a bunch of them to, like, the women's coffeehouse or the Holly Near concert and then the others could be to Key West, Provincetown, San Francisco, or—the real humdinger—an Olivia cruise. And of course we would want to have celebrity guests from time to time, like Martina Navratilova and Rita Mae Brown (though not at the same time, of course) or any one of countless women's music stars, past and present—I'm putting in a vote right now for Tracy Chapman.

The other key ingredient in "The Dating Game," as we all remember—aside from the contestants—are the questions. Being a happily partnered gal myself, I won't be needing them, but I thought maybe I would help you single gals out: "Dykette number 1. Look at Dykette number 2. Describe her to me as if she were a motorcycle." And, "Dykette number 2—if I were a hot fudge sundae, how would you eat me?" Or, "Dykette number 3—if you could be any article of clothing in my drawer, what would you be and why?"

Oh sure, I know: you'd like to write your own questions, give them that personal flair. But how about just a *few* more suggestions? Like, "Dykette number 3. If our first date were a softball field, what play would you be: a line drive, a fumble, a sacrifice fly, or a fast pitch?" Or, "Dykette number 1. If you were a music festival, which one would you be: the Southern Music and Comedy Festival, SisterFire, RhythmFest, or, the mother of all festivals, Michigan?"

The truth is, of course, I'm still evading the problem here: how to stretch that one date into a veritable multitude of dates. Maybe what we lack is a sense of definition. Just what is the *purpose* of dating? Someone who is good at dating, who has a natural feel for the concept—she would indubitably tell you there is no *purpose*. Or if there is a purpose, that purpose is to have fun. Period. But as a self-appointed representative of the average lesbian, I am here to tell you what we all know: the purpose of dating is *to find out if you want to be in a relationship with the other person.*

It is from this, I think, that our sense of futility

concerning dating comes. Here's what I mean: On the off chance that this person is, in fact, the woman of your dreams, you are on your best behavior and are out to impress her. She, no doubt, is pretty much operating in the same manner. The point is, how can you possibly get to know someone when you never get to see her wearing the same torn, stained sweats for an entire weekend? When you don't spend an hour or more searching the store's shelves for a video that will elicit more than a shoulder shrug and facial twitch from her? When she hasn't yet begun releasing to you items from The List of Things She Won't Eat? On my first date with my girlfriend, we set out to an Indian restaurant and then, on finding it closed, went on to a Thai restaurant. Months into our relationship, I discovered she hates Indian food and isn't terribly crazy about Thai. When I related this story to my friend Laura, she guffawed knowingly. "Hah! On the first date, they'll eat octopus." Heck, some women have been known to sleep on a *futon* trying to impress a woman! What I'm aiming at here is that you may be getting to know someone when you're dating all right, but it's not necessarily the same person you may live with someday.

Which brings me to another problem we gals seem to have: living in the moment. Instead, we have a tendency to put the house before the courtship, if you will. One or two dates into "the thing," and "the thing" has inflated like bread dough, in our hot little brains, from a date or two into a relationship. Here's how you know that's happened: instead of planning things like, oh, say, dinner or dancing, you start planning things like vacations, Christmas, dogs, babies, houses. Here's another hint: when you don't know if your sweater, bathrobe, k.d. lang

CD, *Dream of a Common Language,* toothbrush, high tops, softball mitt, and red suit jacket are at your place or hers, you are no longer dating—this may start within a month of your meeting. Well, perhaps it is only I who am so suggestible, but I blame this conflation of time and my fluidity of imagination on Hollywood movies.

Personally, I have always loved those old movies, the dramas and romantic comedies, the ones starring Deborah Kerr and Robert Mitchum, Lana Turner and Robert Forsythe, the ones starring Tracy and Hepburn, Cary Grant—even Rock Hudson and Doris Day. I'm not the kind of movie fan, though, who can talk directors and studios—often I can't even tell you which plots go with which titles or who was in what—I'm just a real sucker for those sappy love stories. It never even really bothered me that they were incredibly heterosexual—this was not, to the best of my recollection, because I identified with the male lead, though I'm sure that did happen some. Rather, it was more that, even before I was really aware of my sexual identity, the translation from heterosexual to lesbian had become second nature—like a native bilingual speaker, translating effortlessly between two different realities.

Unfortunately, I saw so many of these movies that I began to believe *life* was like that—or, at least, if not, that it *could* be. While I'm sure many things about the movies hooked me and reeled me in, six things stand out in my mind about those movies that turned me into the Hollywood-love junkie I am today.

The Happy Ending

The romantic comedies were far and away the films most frequently guilty of the happy ending. Dramas, in fact, generally ended tragically but nobly, which made them all that much more poignant—but more on that later.

In the romantic comedies, no matter how much the romantic leads disliked each other, no matter what outrageous circumstances kept them apart, they always ended up together. Even the occasional drama showed us lovers who, tragically separated, were once again reunited.

What the happy ending has done to me is made me hope against all odds—and against all appearances to the contrary—that things will "work out" in the end. And what *hope* does to me is make me an idiot: that is, it's not that I question reality but that reality, as a concept, is totally outside of my comprehension. So what that she's just gotten involved with someone else; so what if she hasn't called me in two months; so what if she's moved to Seattle, changed her name to Bark Swampfrog, and condemned monogamous relationships as patriarchal; so what if she's thinking about becoming a nun—it'll all come out the way it's *supposed* to. Well, I hate to say it, but until recently I was strongly beginning to suspect that I got Ingmar Bergman for my scriptwriter instead of Kauffmann and Hart! (even if they are playwrights, not screenwriters).

Love at First Sight

This is an ailment of epidemic proportions in the lesbian community (the point of this whole diatribe, in fact) and could single-handedly keep a fleet of moving vans in business. Fortunately for me, my love-at-first-sight "relationships" have seldom advanced to the moving-in-together stage. Consequently, the logistics are somewhat easier when one or both of us realize we have no idea who this woman is we've been sleeping with. Even so, it always comes as a painful surprise as, in general, love at first sight in the movies is almost always love for life. Let's put it this way: because of the movies, I don't believe in love at first sight—I expect it.

The Persistent Lover

This is the would-be lover who won't take no for an answer and constantly follows, calls, and generally harasses the intended. In the movies, this obsessive persistence is either cute and funny or incredibly touching (and always pays off, of course). In real life, it is neurotic and/or obnoxious. Can you say "stalking," girls and girls?

The Charm of Romance

Another thing Hollywood has ingrained in me is that if you're romantic enough, you can charm the key ring off a dyed-in-the-cords butch. Well, that's not *exactly* the message I got from the movies—it's my rough translation. So I learned to be romantic as hell—not just your basic flowers and cards routine but also the more exotic, creative kind of package: a box of graham crackers (or whatever) because she mentioned once that she liked them; a late night picnic with wine, crackers, cheese, and fruit; a loaf of homemade bread; a love poem written just for her; an autograph from her favorite movie star; a surprise visit during the middle of the work day, and so on. I *love* romance! However, what I've learned is that *(1)* unless she's already attracted to you, such behavior can scare and/or annoy the hell out of her, and *(2)* just cuz you're of a romantic nature doesn't mean you can expect reciprocity. It doesn't matter though: I'm addicted, in love—with romance.

The Silent Sufferer

This one, of course, comes from the dramas—no one is ever silent in romantic comedies, where everyone is always quick with snappy repartee, witty dialogue, and biting wisecracks. In the dramas, though, there were often traumatic occurrences, tragedies, or terrible misunderstandings that separated two people who it was *obvious* were meant to be together. This, naturally, resulted primarily in sad, quiet acceptance from one or both parties—terribly heart-rending. My all-time favorite of this genre is *Madame X* with Lana Turner—it never fails to cause me to go through half a box of tissues on every viewing. This high drama with all of its noble suffering and sadness in the name of love was very appealing to me for a long time—the movies always made it seem so romantic and beautiful. Thankfully, I've finally outgrown this one and decided that suffering sucks.

Destiny

This is the sense that two people were meant to be with one another—and only one another—forever and, no matter what happens, eventually will be. I've had this sense about myself and another many times. Consequently, I have in the past spent months (which have added up to years) waiting patiently for the inevitable. Up until quite recently, however, all of my leading ladies had different scriptwriters.

And now that I have miraculously—just like in a movie—found the woman of my dreams, I am convinced we are starring in a wacky romantic comedy. When I'm feeling grandiose, I think of us as a sort of Hepburn-Tracy combo. In more rational moments, though, I suspect we really have more in common with Lucy and Ethel.

Anyway, you can see how using Hollywood movies as a guide to dating, to relationships—to life—might create something of a problem. I don't know about anyone else, but I'd say that's the case with me. When I think now of dating, either in the abstract or my experience of it, a shiver runs up and down my slightly curved little spine. Come to think of it, dating is a lot like a B-grade horror flick: lots of suspense and a little bit scary, with a predictable plot.

And perhaps one of *the* most frightening times in the dating process is when you first sleep together. Let me be clear here: I'm not even talking about anything having to do with sex, which holds thrills and anxieties all its own. No, I'm speaking, now, of the simple act of sleeping. Simple though it may be, letting someone that you're dying to impress see you before, during, and after sleep requires a tremendous amount of courage.

First of all, there are things you may do in your sleep that you have no way of knowing—unless someone (hopefully someone who loves you very much) has told you about the things you do when you're unconscious. Does your mouth, for instance, hang open, allowing your tongue to expand over your lower lip like warm bread dough? Are your exhalations or inhalations plagued by mysterious assorted whistles, grunts, and snorts? Do you say revealing things in your sleep, like "Hurry! There's a blue-light special on knee-high nylons!" Or, "Hillary, Hillary—leave Bill and run away with me."

But perhaps even more frightening are the things you *know* you do—and can do nothing to control. Take twitching, for example. You know—that sensation when you're just about asleep, and even though your body's in bed, your mind is walking down the street and trips over a crack in the sidewalk, causing your entire body, which is still in the bed, to brace itself for the fall. That's what I mean by twitching. And even though all of us do it (right? or have I just said something revealing about myself?), it's somehow embarrassing when you do it in bed with someone you don't know all that well.

Still, that's a fairly minor embarrassment. Imagine instead, if you will, this scenario: You're asleep. Your head rests on the shoulder of your beloved. You are enfolded in loving arms while your eyes flicker in REM sleep. You snuggle in a little closer and—yikes! You are awakened as your face slides into the already cooling puddle of drool that you left in the hollow of your lover's shoulder. Well. You only have to wake up like that once—or even on your own drool-dampened pillow alone—to be wary of *ever* falling asleep again in the presence of another. This, my friends, is the true source of insomnia.

Even if you manage to make it through the night, the scary part's not over yet. While waking up with someone next to you can be one of the greatest of the simple pleasures, the first few times with someone can be anxiety-producing. I am, of course, referring to that well-known trilogy of terror: morning mouth, big hair, and crusty eyes. (I shudder at the mere writing of these words.) Having multicolored mineral deposits is not the only way your eyes can betray you on these first mornings, either. Those of us who can't see a thing until we don spectacles or contacts have been known to squint adoringly—and most attractively, I'm sure—at the fine features of our newly beloved. And if you're lucky, and it's summertime, you may be able to add a fourth to the terrifying trio: hayfever. There's nothing quite so provocative as a furious Uzi-like firing of sneezes, accompanied by several delicate honks of one's hooter and the ensuing balled up soggy tissues.

The good thing about these terrors of the sleep is that, if someone sticks with you after they have borne witness to your red-splotched pillow-imprinted face, you know she loves you for more than your natural good looks. But even if you make it through these early areas of fright, you're not done with sleep issues. As you settle into the relationship—after your second or third date—you discover a whole range of different approaches the two of you have to sleeping and waking. There's getting up early versus sleeping in; sleeping on the right side versus sleeping on the left side; and how many blankets it takes to keep things at a comfortable temperature for both of you. Morning foodstuffs are also part of the sleeping/waking continuum. Take coffee, for example. While I generally wake in sleepy good humor, my lover has been known to be borderline homicidal before her morning cup of coffee. [Note to myself: be sure she doesn't see this passage before that first cup of java.] Okay, so she's not really that bad—she just needs a little caffeine to jump-start herself in the morning. As for breakfast, we're pretty much opposites on this issue as well. For me, the sooner after waking I am able to ingest something hot and gooey (oh stop!), the better. Kathy, on the other hand, prefers to let a decent interval of time pass before getting involved with a meal.

When you reach the juncture in the relationship when you start talking about moving in together, the biggest sleep issue of all may come up: What kind of bed should you have? Basically, there are three choices: conventional, futon, or water. Futon versus waterbed is one of the longest running arguments—preceded only by the cat versus dog controversy—in the lesbian community. (Combine these two for hours of fun: Will the cat/dog be allowed on the futon/waterbed?) When I met Kathy, she was strictly a futon kind of gal; now she says I've ruined her for anything but a waterbed. (All part of a bigger plan, Kath.) Even if you're both conventional folks, I've heard you can have your differences as well—for example, soft? Or firm? Electric blanket? Or long underwear?

Anyway, if you can figure out how, literally, to sleep with someone else, you should be well on your way toward developing a waking relationship with her too. Still, let's face it: there are way too many variables involved in modern-day lesbian courtship. And the only thing I can tell you for sure is, I'm glad *I'm* not dating anymore. . . .

Here At The Grand Coulee Dental Dam

I've got to be honest with you: just the thought of writing about sex makes me nervous. I did not come from one of those progressive households where sex was considered healthy and normal and the subject of intelligent conversation and where the human body was just another part of nature. In my house, I never even saw anyone in their *underwear,* and my stepfather was so squeamish about anything that hinted of sex that if the subject of pregnancy ever came up on television, the channel was changed. My first therapist actually said to me once, "Somewhere inside of you, there's a nun trying to get out." I think she meant I was too sex shy even for a nun, but I was so busy contemplating how a nun got into my little Protestant body that I never gave it serious thought.

This is not to say that I am averse to sex. It's just that chatting casually about sex is not second nature to me. *On Our Backs,* Pat Califia, sex toy parties—the mere mention of any such pro-sex icons causes me to blush like a virgin. I am no Susie Bright, lesbian sex maven. I am not even Susie Dull. I am Sister Betrille. (Yikes! It's that nun-thing again.) As you might guess, I am not a member of the Sex Positive Movement. I am positive I like sex, but I positively don't want to talk about it. That's about as close as I get to membership. Personally, I have nothing against this movement; I think it's a fine and lovely one. But you have to bear in mind that I come from an era in which Rob and Laura Petrie slept in separate beds and no explanation whatsoever was forthcoming as to how it was little Richie came to be. I still suspect he was adopted.

This reticence on my part to talk the lingo of lovemaking has had an impact on several areas of my life. Take therapy, for instance. On the one or two occasions when I thought I should discuss a . . . sexual thing, it has been no problem for me to fill an entire hour stuttering, studying my shoelace, muttering phrases like "down . . . there" and "when she, you know. . . ," tugging at my collar, and clearing my throat, in which anything resembling intelligible sentences have apparently become lodged. When the therapist—bless her soul—tries to intercede and give me some direction by asking a specific question, it suddenly becomes urgent that I doublecheck that the wall to my left does, in fact, connect to the ceiling, following which it is important to determine that the window is still there on my right, where last I saw it.

During such sessions, a 7'x9' room becomes infinitely architecturally interesting.

As you might imagine, this amatory inarticulateness also has an effect on my love-making. When I was involved with men, this wasn't really a problem because not only was talking unnecessary, it was hardly even important for me to be there. With women, however, sex is more of a participatory event. I generally hope that I can get by using my extraordinary powers of ESP. I like to operate under the premise that my partner and I are, like, so spiritually connected we will each just *know* what the other one wants. I am encouraged in this belief by the fact that either the vast majority of my past partners have held similar beliefs or they were just too darn polite to say anything. And somehow, by golly, we did manage to muddle our way through with loving little directional shoves, subtle shifts of the body, and meaningful, encouraging grunts.

In my experience, this technique of sexual communication is especially prevalent between women who are exploring intimacy together for the first time, at least in part because you don't want to give her the impression, by talking like a longshoreman on leave, that sex is more than just a hobby for you. Also influencing this tendency is the Hollywood-generated myth of perfect sex the first time, every time. In fact, though, I have generally found first-time sex more like Rubik's cube: a lot of twisting and turning trying to get everything lined up right without ever quite succeeding. What gets you through that initial fit of passion, I think, is momentum. It's like a roller coaster ride at an amusement park: once you're going, you have no choice but to enjoy all the thrills and chills—

only there's a lot less screaming in sex. Unless, of course, you're that type.

Sexual attraction can be like an electromagnet: one minute you're a sane person, the next your body is crazy glued to someone else's. The night my girlfriend and I originally experienced this phenomenon, we were not at a place in our lives where we wanted to be physically involved with one another. Thus, each time we found our bodies sucked together, we struggled to pull apart. So overpowering was this pull that Kathy at some point lost sight of why it was we felt a need to stop ourselves from going in the direction we were clearly headed: "What are we, nuns? Suburban housewives?"

Still, there *are* ways of breaking the mood. I recall one time, much further along in our relationship, when Kath and I were in an amorous mood. Sitting on the edge of the bed, we kissed, and as we grew more impassioned, we fell back into a prone position. Shortly thereafter, Kathy paused from kissing my neck to say, "Your shirt smells like Pounce." No, Pounce is neither, as you may be thinking, a fabric softener nor the latest cologne from Elizabeth Taylor but, rather, an edible cat treat. Hardly stopping to ponder the strangeness of this, I gallantly removed my shirt and we picked up where we had left off. But again Kathy was distracted. "You still smell like Pounce," she announced, though she needn't have—for precisely at that moment I rolled into the puddle of cat barf cooling on the bedspread. Now *that* is guaranteed to kill the moment.

But to return to my tongue-tiedness, so to speak, on the subject of sex, I would have been in serious trouble if my sexual awakening had occurred during the advent of AIDS. I would probably have become a nun, religious barrier or no religious barrier, before I would have had the gumption to raise the subject of dental dams. Though come to think of it, what with the convent running rampant with "particular friends" and all, I guess such a conversion wouldn't necessarily preclude a sex life. . . .

As it is, it's a good thing I've been in a long-term committed union for some time now, though I know that even that is no guarantee of safety. Still, in terms of our past lives, it's a little late *now,* at this advanced date in our relationship, to protect against that. In terms of future extracurricular activities, Kath and I are so monogamous, we don't even have sex with each other—just with ourselves. Kidding! I am totally kidding. But I mean it when I say how much I admire the Sex Positive generation of younger dykes and their straightforwardness in openly yacking it up about all things erotic, including safer sex. To them, dental dams are just a natural part of sex; to me, stuttering is a natural part of sex.

In any case, you have to admit that the concept of dental dams is a strange one. The object of dental dams, of course, is to put a protective barrier between your mouth and her lips, if you get my drift, but I would like to have been there with whoever came up with this idea. Whatever caused him—and given the overall inadequacy of the thing, you know it wasn't a woman's invention—to take a rarely used *dental* tool and move it to the complete opposite end of the body? It's like putting the leash on the tail-end of the dog. One thing I have to say for dental dams, though, is they give an entirely new meaning to that old Girl Scout song that goes, "I have something in my pocket, it belongs across my face. . . ." Also, surprisingly enough, given how inconvenient they are in other ways, dental dams are eminently portable. Just slip one in your pocket and you're ready to go—which causes the phrase "Is that a dental dam in your pocket, or are you just happy to see me?" to spring to mind. On second thought, given the recommendation that dental dams be stored in a cool place, perhaps it's not such a good idea to keep one in your pocket . . . *especially* when venturing out on a hot date.

Plastic wrap works well for safer sex too—and, it's probably right there in your kitchen. In fact, I'm surprised the plastic wrap people haven't jumped on this in their ad campaigns as another reason to buy their product: "Safe, from the freezer to the bedroom: Handiwrap." Anyway, after you wrap up that leftover tofu cutlet, it's ever so easy to take it along with you on your date—the plastic wrap, not the cutlet, although you may find the latter handy too if you suddenly need a dose of protein. Watch the serrated edge, though, when stuffing the box in your pocket. Aside from the convenience of plastic wrap over dental dams, it requires much less precision; I don't know about you, but in the heat of the moment, pinpoint control is not one of my strong points. But heck, with a roll of plastic wrap, you could go hog wild. It's nice, too, that it lets you actually see what's under its protective barrier—unless, of course, you go in for those new-fangled fashion colors in your food wrap.

There was some concern about microwave plastic wrap and whether it was too permeable to be safe, but the Centers for Disease Control say it's safe up to temperatures of 144°F. So, unless you're having *really* hot sex, you should be okay. I suspect that even though it's a regular household object it would not be any easier for *me* to introduce it at a delicate moment, although now I know why they call it Glad Wrap.

In spite of my own shyness, I can especially see the significance of candid safer sex talk when S/M is involved. Although it's true that I once derived the slogan "A little S/M never hurt anyone," the closest I have gotten—and hope ever to get—to such an encounter is this: Once, on a second date, I spotted a pair of handcuffs hanging on my date's bedroom wall. I thought it was an interesting wall decoration but did not ponder it further. Later, we somehow got on the topic of S/M. "I don't understand how hurting someone can be a sign of love," I said to this woman.

"I don't either," she responded. "But if someone *wanted* me to whip them, I'd whip them." After a pause, she added pensively, "When you think about it, sex in a chair is really dumb. But if you're *tied* to the chair. . . ." That the handcuffs were more than an artistic statement became disturbingly clear to me.

Being the fair-minded kind of gal I am, I can see how S/M might spice up the old sex life after you've been with someone a long time. I don't mean to imply that caressing the love of your life gets boring, but after a number of years, there aren't all that many surprises. Still, I think that, personally, a whip crack across the back is a surprise I'd be willing to forgo. Why not wow her instead with a dildo? There are ample choices of size, color, and shape from which to choose. Although I have to admit this is yet another area I don't have a lot of experience in, my own feeling is that the flesh-colored realistic kind, with the veins and all, are more than a little creepy, especially after the whole Lorena Bobbitt thing. But to each her own.

Also not on the top of my list for dildo selections would be a Barbie doll. In fact, I would never have even thought of her as an option if it hadn't been for the *On*

Our Backs Cover Dyke a few years ago who mentioned Barbie as her toy of choice. Since then, Barbie cum dildo (if you'll pardon the expression) has been on my mind. I puzzle over questions like, Was she inserted head first? Or feet first? With her arms up? Or down? Wouldn't those tiny plastic fingers poke and scratch? (And not in a good way.) Does all that hair tickle? I also wondered if she varied which type of Barbie she used—Malibu Barbie vs. Rock Star Barbie vs. Nurse Barbie—depending on her mood, but then I realized the Barbies probably weren't wearing clothes at the time, and without outfits on, aren't all Barbies really the same? Even Black Barbie has the same anorexic figure and white-girl hair. In any case, I certainly hope that if Barbie was jumping in feet first she didn't have her diminutive plastic heels on. You could lose those puppies in there forever. Imagine the doctor's surprise at *that* woman's next gyne exam. . . .

Another word of caution: if you use Dildo Barbie with multiple partners, you should really have her wear a condom for safety's sake. When I think about this, the image that comes to mind is Bonnie Blair in her sleek little skating outfit—which puts a whole new spin on the fantasy elements of the endeavor and adds piquancy to the phrase "Going for the gold." Maybe Mattel (or whoever has to take the blame for Barbie) could help things along in this area by marketing a Scuba-Diving Barbie, which would come packaged already pretty much dildo encased.

A more conventional but very popular choice for putting electricity back into a relationship is the vibrator. If you have your pick among gas-powered, electric, and battery-operated, I say go for the last one. Even though electric is very environmentally friendly, the cord is bound to get in the way, and the gas-powered is so noisy, in addition to all the fumes you have to contend with. Furthermore, with the latter choice, if you're the type to light up a cigarette after sex, you could get more bang for your buck than you bargained for.

When you're dealing with appliances, there are bound to be problems no matter what. One lesbian couple I heard about checked into a hotel room while on vacation. As the bellhop was showing them around the room, they noticed an annoying hum coming from the TV and asked for a new room. No sooner were they in their next quarters than they noticed the refrigerator was whining. They called the front desk and again asked to be moved. In the third room, they also noticed an unpleasant noise and started searching the room for its source. It seemed to be coming from one of their suitcases. Much to their embarrassment, they discovered their vibrator had gotten switched on during travel. I don't think they shared this story with the hotel management.

That's why I like to limit myself to the parts I came with during those intimate moments. Though at this stage of my life, it may be time for Kathy to call in reinforcements of the inanimate kind. Let's just say that it's a good thing she's younger than me because, even so, I test her stamina. It won't be long before she will need to take breaks, part way through, to carb up. I think that's why it's been so long since the last time we made love: Kathy is still resting up. She's also intensifying her work-out routine in preparation for next time. Don't get me wrong: we both love wallowing in the moment. But when "the moment" lasts longer than a seventeen-inning baseball game, well, it might be time to call in a relief pitcher, one that's fresh and new—and battery-operated. For now, though, I think we are perfectly content with our own meditative style of love-making: a slow and reverent pilgrimage to some holy place—with a lot of Hosannahs at the end. It's our own little version of speaking in tongues.

Sure, I joke about sex. But it's only so I can avoid actually talking about it. Sometimes, however, talking about it is pretty much unavoidable. Like the time Kathy and I went to the JoAnn Loulan sex workshop. What was I *thinking?* Oh I remember: it was free. Frugality—along with prudishness—is the other thing I inherited from my family. Because Kathy helped produce JoAnn's show in Chicago, we had the opportunity of attending not only her show but also the workshop. For all I know, the entire workshop was memorable and useful, but I can't be certain because I was so traumatized by the part where we were divided up into groups of three couples and sent off to talk—*over lunch*—about the specifics of our sex lives that all of the preceding events are now entirely lost to me.

JoAnn's instructions went something like: "Tell what you like to do sexually, where you like to do it, and so on." I hadn't even told these things to *Kath*y—how was I supposed to articulate them to total strangers over a plate of rusty head lettuce? Because of a loud thumping sound emanating from the vicinity of my chest, I have no idea what anyone else said at lunch. In fact, I don't even remember what either Kathy or I said, although I do have a dim recollection of us somehow deftly steering the conversation to much less intimate topics of partnership, like how you handle finances or who you have in mind for a semen donor.

My only consolation about the total affair—after having mumbled my way through the typical series of "You knows" and "Um, down theres"—was that most likely I would never see any of these women again. A week or two later, of course, while visiting a friend of mine, I discovered one of the couples we had lunch with was her upstairs tenant. Personally, I find it hard to converse casually with someone whose most vivid image of you, formed during a luncheon conversation, involves your face being partially obscured by someone else's thigh. I did learn one thing from the experience, though: it's very hard to swallow a bite of grilled cheese sandwich when someone has her metaphoric tongue "down there."

My level of comfort with sex talk is not increasing, either, with advancing years. That circumstance, coupled with the fact that Kathy and I are just now, after almost seven years, beginning to work out a complex system of codes and signals that makes us *feel* as though we're communicating intelligibly but would be gibberish to anyone else, leads me to cherish monogamy more than ever. All that, and the certitude that I am still crazy in love enough with Kathy to fill those idle hours fruitfully with just the one gal, thank you very much. Besides, I've got all the latex products in my life right now that I care to have. Which reminds me: those dishes are still in the sink. . . .

The Marrying Kind

Some gals love the swingin' singles scene: the excitement, the adventure, the independence, the variety, the freedom. Me? I'm the marrying kind.

These are surprising words to be coming from me, someone who was never particularly enchanted with the traditional institution of marriage. While my peers were reading *Bride* magazine and spinning elaborate fantasies about gowns and rings and dancing to "Proud Mary," I was looking for a softball team. Nevertheless, I did discover, over time, that while visions of myself with a veil over my face didn't rise unbidden to my mind, I *was* interested in settling down into legal spinsterhood with a companion of similar proclivities and exactly the same gender.

This is a daring stance to take these days, what with

anticouples caucuses springing up all over the gay and lesbian community. However, I am no stranger to danger: I once rode my bike down a flight of stairs and, scarier yet, I played on a softball team one summer with *two* of my ex-lovers, plus a woman I had unsuccessfully courted. So I know all about taking risks.

Nevertheless, I stand my ground: I am happy to be in a long-term committed relationship. Not that being part of a couple is one Kodak moment after another. As with any couple, there are all the usual problems and pitfalls, many of them pretty much the same no matter what your sexual orientation. But lesbian and gay couples also have some unique problems. When was the last time, for instance, you saw a lesbian couple on the *Newlywed Game*? There just isn't the same kind of celebration of and support for homosexual unions as there is for heterosexual ones.

Oh sure, we have domestic partnership benefits where I work—and, boy, do we feel that our love is so much more sanctified now that the Human Resources Department has recognized it—but I have my doubts about how hard the in-laws would fight to keep us together if we ever thought of going our separate ways. Mostly, though, it's the everyday stuff that can wear a body down. It ain't easy keeping the romance alive.

To begin with, there are a lot of things about the human body that are just plain gross. You know what I'm talking about: you know what you do in the privacy of your own home. Well, when you're dating—our own weird little human mating ritual—you go to great lengths to make it seem as though your only bodily functions are kissing, orgasm, and smiling inanely. But there's only so long you can keep up that pretense. Eventually, you are going to get gas.

Now I'll grant you that I may be a lot more squeamish about these things than most. In fact, I have known a lot of people who are much more comfortable with the body's products than I. A woman I used to date, for instance, took tremendous pride in being able to burp the alphabet—the key words here being *used to*. But the gist of the matter is, while familiarity may not breed contempt, it sure as heck breeds something—and it's not always something romantic, which can make it a real challenge to resuscitate that element of your coupling.

Here's how it happens: basically, as your relationship progresses, you begin to relax more and more in the presence of your lover. This is as it should be. I believe the insanity rate would go up exponentially if people had to pretend, twenty-four hours a day for every day of their lives, that they never got food stuck in that back upper molar, food that could only be dislodged by excavation with a fingernail, preferably their own. I'm not saying one should go around belching like Mount Vesuvius about to erupt, but you gotta loosen up a little. If feeling at ease with one another is in any way the hallmark of a successful relationship, then, woowee, you just can't get more successful than soaking your menstrual-stained undies in the sink, not showering for a whole weekend while you're doing household repairs, or being there to assist for various minor "medical" procedures, such as zit patrol and the eradication and extraction of an in-grown hair in her armpit with a tweezers.

And what isn't gross, after a couple of years, is merely mundane. Gift giving, for instance, may not be as fanciful as it once was. A friend of mine recently confessed to me at Christmas that she was running out of "toys" to buy her lover, having purchased gifts, over the eight years they'd been together, of everything from a mini-bike to a video camera to exercise machines. Another friend confided that for the first time in seven years she and her lover had broken down and bought underwear for each other for Christmas. And we're not talking something lacy, black, silky, and sexy, either—something you might see in that soft-core porn mag that passes for a Victoria's Secret Catalog. No: we're talking old-fashioned plain ol' cotton undies.

Now I don't want you to mistake what I'm doing here for complaining. I am not complaining at all. I am just documenting the cold hard facts of reality because, dammit, that's my job! Actually, I am quite relieved not to have dating-related anxiety all the time about what sort of impression I'm making: What if she's repulsed by my Ed Grimly-like morning hair? How will I know if it's okay to smile after eating this corn on the cob? Oh-oh: I think my deodorant just went out on a wildcat strike. No, I'm glad that's over. There's a lot to be said for being secure enough in a relationship to know her love goes deeper than that crusty thing in the corner of your eye right now.

There are, of course, other trying things about maintaining a relationship besides the less endearing bodily functions. One such thing is summer.

Summer might not be a problem for folks who live in a climate-controlled environment, like astronauts or Samson down at the zoo. There's something, though, about undergoing a week or more at a stretch where the thermostat in the house never dips below 89°F—causing the space between one's breasts to look like a waterslide—that causes my partner and me to have personality meltdowns. This sort of thing tends to be bad for a relationship. Therefore, in the summer of '91, when the words "greenhouse effect" were never far from our parched lips, we developed a strategy for beating the heat—in other words, for saving our relationship. Here I pass along to you our collected wisdom.

1. Spend time in shopping malls. The key here, as with so many of our other acts of desperation that summer, was the air conditioning. We liked to think of these excursions as cultural experiences, like visiting a foreign country. Did you know it is fashionable to make your bangs stand straight up in the air? This comes as quite a shock to those of us who grew up in the fifties and sixties, those of us who were taught that bangs should lie tidily on our foreheads. My own mother used some sort of goo on my hair called DuSharm to achieve the desired tidiness. Near as I can recollect, it seemed to have been some sort of grease enhancer. Anyway, my girlfriend and I, whilst wandering among the giant potted plants, would try not to get freaked out by all the Metallica and Let's-Kill-Them-All-And-Let-God-Sort-Them-Out t-shirts so we could still enjoy the high point of the evening: frozen yogurt.

2. Go to the movies. The lure, again, was the air conditioning. This tends to be better than going to the malls because, for the most part, you don't actually have to *look* at the people around you. Nevertheless, their presence can still be palpable. During one movie, for example, the woman behind us tsked and moaned sympathetically throughout the entire movie. You might think we were seeing a movie like, maybe, *Dying Young*. But no, the movie in question was *City Slicker*s—a comedy.

3. Take lots of long, cool baths. This is remarkably bracing. And the advantage is, you don't have to see any guys with beer bellies and sweat-stained baseball caps, and the only moaning you'll hear is your own. (I meant that metaphorically.) The disadvantage with this solution, at least with our tub, is that it only seats one. And by the time the second bather has partaken, the first one is already hot, sweaty, and disagreeable again.

4. Hang out with your girlfriend's parents. Depending on your lover's parents, you might be thinking, "Hey, I thought these were ways to *beat* the heat, not make it worse." Let me tell you—there's something mighty appealing about my girlfriend's parents: central air. Still, I have to admit this was perhaps our most desperate act. We were so desperate, in fact, that we willingly listened while Kathy's dad talked about some arcane detail of the stock broker biz that completely eluded me. I smiled and nodded a lot, feigning rapt attention but was actually concentrating, on the damp stickiness leaving my skin.

5. Buy a five-dollar pool—you know, the little inflatable kind? You can't exactly dive in and do laps, but you can slide your legs into the icy water, fresh out of the garden hose. This has a surprisingly overall cooling effect. We would pull our lawn chairs up of an evening and have drinks by the pool. The neighbors looked at us kind of funny, but hey, we're used to that by now. Of course, if you're lawnless, the pool option presents some rather formidable problems, such as how to drain it. Unless, that is, the previous tenant in your apartment was a lowland gorilla who had tiles and drains installed in the living room for ease of cleaning. Or unless you know a lot of really thirsty and kind of kinky people willing to come in with straws after you're done reclining in the aforementioned pool. If you don't have recourse to either of these pool-draining resources, you'd probably be best off skipping directly to option 6.

6. Weasel dinner out of your friends who speak softly but carry a big air-conditioning unit. I suggest doing this sparingly though. More than once or twice a week, and they may begin to suspect you only love them for their freon.

7. Lie naked in front of the fan and spritz each other with water. This is très refreshing but somewhat limits your activity. Visits from the precinct captain or an old high-school buddy, for instance, are ill-advised at this time.

8. Hang out in the basement. Okay, I confess: we didn't actually do this. But it *could* be a good idea if the basement where you live wasn't a National Parks refuge for spiders and millipedes and if it didn't have a ceiling height designed with the inhabitants of Oz in mind.

When I look back on those punishingly hot days now, it all seems like a bad acid-rain trip. But I know it must have been real because I keep finding movie-ticket stubs in my pockets; because there are, in the garage, purple and orange hippos dancing around the inflated ring of a pool; and because words like "secondaries," "cyclicals," and "Ginnie Maes" keep rising like gas bubbles to my conscious mind.

Summer isn't the only season, though, to raise the tension level in an otherwise happy, healthy lesbian household. There is also the fifth season, so often forgotten when cataloging the other four. I refer, of course, to the holiday season—the Tito Jackson of seasons, if you will. And when people do talk about the holiday season, frequently it is to complain about how stressful it is. As tension filled as this season is for hetero couples, it can be just that much more so for gay and lesbian couples.

When a friend of mine asked, a while back, if my lover and I had worked out the holidays yet, I knew she wasn't referring to a new Jane Fonda video for vanquishing all those unwanted pounds from too many spiked eggnogs, pfefferneuse, and buttered slices of stollen. No, "working out the holidays," I knew, had to do with a preholiday ritual rather than a postholiday one. She was referring, of course, to the decision-making process surrounding who celebrates what with whom, where, and when.

Take Christmas, for example. If you and/or your lover and/or either of your families are into Christmas, you are unavoidably thrown into the St. Nick talks, a sort of domestic version of the SALT Talks, only with less diplomacy. If you're not out to your family yet, these talks can get particularly convoluted and bizarre: "I know it's unusual, Mom, but I have a very important volleyball tournament Christmas eve so I won't be able to make it home. My team is counting on me!" Even if your family knows you're a lesbian, there's not necessarily full recognition of your relationship. "Sure, bring her along Christmas eve. Aunt Sissy and Uncle Steve's neighbors will be there, so that'll be fine. But Christmas dinner, gee, that's just for family, dear. . . ." At which point—well, let's just say: so much for peace on earth. Or at least on your block.

But forget about all these family negotiations: we've got holiday problems of our own, just the two of us. Like dealing with the Christmas tree. You might think two gals like us, with our good liberal politics and our concern about the environment, wouldn't be needlessly slaughtering a helpless piece of living timber for a few days of pagan revelry with a few dashes of Christianity thrown in for the purists. But neither our consciences nor our past experience with the Christmas tree gestalt has stopped us from indulging in this time-honored tradition.

For us, actually, the whole tree thing is the focal point of the holidays. In fact, when we were house hunting,

Kathy formed her opinions on the suitability of each house in part on the basis of where we would put the Christmas tree. But this is not terribly surprising from someone who now says she wants to move because we don't get enough trick-or-treaters at Halloween, which is actually her favorite holiday. As much as we love our tannenbaum, it has been known to raise the holiday stress level in our household a good notch or two over the years.

Our first year, for instance, as we were merrily putting on our mittens and scarves getting ready to dash off in my four-horse little Honda, we started what seemed like a harmless enough discussion about our hypothetical child. I'll spare you the details, but imagine, if you will, how such a discussion might go between a lapsed but not thoroughly disenchanted Catholic and a confirmed agnostic. It got kind of ugly, with words and phrases creeping into the conversation like "heathen," "religious mumbo-jumbo," and "Sunday Mass." My main regret, though, is how the poor tree had to suffer as a consequence, being roughly thrown into the back of the car, then unceremoniously dumped against a wall in the apartment.

What is truly surprising, though, is that we managed to select a tree at all, given our different species preferences. Somehow, I never thought to ask, on the second or third date, if she preferred long needles or short, real trees or fake. And once you get past a month or two, it seems so superficial to dump someone because she likes Scotch pines instead of balsam firs. Luckily, Kathy and I are at least in agreement about the reprehensiblility of artificial trees—our relationship would have been in definite jeopardy if she had insisted on one of those aluminum numbers with the tri-color revolving light—but there is still the needle-length issue to contend with. I am of a mind that long needles are soft and elegant looking; Kath believes short needles are clearly superior. That first year of tree shopping, we were fortunately spared from adding any more emotional content to our tree search—already made passionate by apparently having to plan the entire religious upbringing of a child it now looks like we'll never have—because the long-needled trees were out of our price range. Whose point do you think *that* proves? We handle these things so maturely—a hallmark of our relationship.

Selecting and transporting the tree is only part of the story, as you no doubt know. The next step is to get the beast up in its stand. Anything mechanical, using the simple laws of physics—like, say, turning three screws in such a way as to hold a slender woody plant in an upright position—causes unpleasant personality changes in the two of us. I have had visions of a lonely Christmas, calling all of my much more well-adjusted friends, who would be sipping hot cups of holiday cheer before their stately, erect Christmas trees, and saying to them, "We split up—we couldn't get the tree to stand up straight in the stand."

There are the aesthetics of the decorated tree to consider as well. This is an area that seems rife with possibilities for artistic disagreement. At the risk of sounding boastful, I have to say that Kath and I are always in perfect harmony about when our pine has reached peak beauty. How have we accomplished this almost unheard of feat? *(1)* We are, for the most part, restricted by the collection of lights and ornaments packed away in our mutual Christmas box. We both agree: when the box is empty, the tree is decorated. *(2)* Because of Kathy's allergies to pine needles, *I* do all the decorating; I find I'm pretty congenial with myself about the adornment process.

There is another holiday pitfall we have thus far managed to avoid: succumbing to the romanticism of those places where you can chop down your own tree. Just the thought of the two of us trudging through the snow with a cold December wind gnawing at our cheek bones, wielding an ax with which to drive a wedge into the wood, hoping to fell the tree in a predetermined direction, pulling it along through the underbrush back to the car where we will have to tie the flailing thing to the roof with our numb little fingers—well, the whole scenario makes me shudder simply to contemplate it. We have been known to suffer domestic strife moving the chest of drawers across the bedroom in a cozily heated house; trouncing through the frozen forest in a goal-oriented sort of way does not seem like the best plan for guaranteeing our ongoing connubial bliss.

And that is something I strive to maintain. Most folks, if surveyed, would probably say the same—other than, maybe, a few perversely Rambo-esque alumnae of debate teams. Even so, there are those, whether they would admit it or not, who value the excitement and the appearance of vitality that arguments add to their relationships. Not me. Nosiree: I'd just as soon avoid all that yelling and gnashing of teeth and tear-inducing hullabaloo. And when I can't, I want to get it over with ASAP.

That, of course, is easier said than done. There you are, passionately discussing whose responsibility it was to have cleaned the doggie do out of the backyard–which, incidentally, you just stepped in with your brand new cross-trainers—when the next thing you know, she is reminiscing about the time you borrowed her suede boots—without her permission—and stepped in an oily puddle of water. Impressed by the adeptness with which she traverses down Memory Lane, you share the perception, in an effort to be helpful, "You're just like your mother"—or father, or Nancy Kerrigan, or whoever she most doesn't want to be like but is afraid she is. Alternatively, you might choose to make the equally helpful observation: "Well, that's just what I'd expect from someone who would go out with [insert name of most reprehensible ex-lover here]." Statements such as these, as you know from past experience, are likely to bring up a few "issues," as we lesbians are fond of saying—issues that haven't been resolved in twenty or thirty years and aren't likely to be in the next half hour, even with your oh-so-considerate guidance.

Some arguments, though, are particularly tricky to resolve at all, let alone in quick fashion. Once, some friends of mine were on an excruciatingly long and difficult road trip. It became apparent at some point to the one who was driving that the other was irritated with her. "What's the matter," she queried, "don't you like my driving?" "I don't like the way you *breathe,*" responded her lover.

In spite of the painfulness of arguments, though, some people like to think of them as little tests of the relationship, or lessons in life. These are the people who perpetually prefer to search for the good in others, who always look on the bright side, who are often described as "perky"—these are the people you'd like to shake brusquely and say, "Cheer down a little, wouldja? Your incessant maturity is unnatural and it's getting to me."

But the people who really worry me are the ones who actually *set out* to test the relationship, however unconsciously. The most popular way to do this in the lesbian community seems to be the extrarelational dalliance, though in truth it's more than a test—it's a pyrotechnic display! This method of appraisal is way too messy for me: you drag in a third person, risk loud scenes in public places, and muddy up the results of your test. On the up side, of course, is the contribution you make to the arts, hence the term "dyke drama."

Personally, I would recommend, for anyone who is feeling the strain of wanting to maintain quality control of her domestic partnership, a method of assessment a little less splashy than creating an isosceles triangle with human points. The way I see it, why introduce an unknown variable (the Other Woman) when there is so much you can discover about the tenor of your union with nothing more than the tools at hand?

For instance—speaking of tools—you could try assembling together a simple piece of machinery such as, oh, say, a rototiller. The test here is not whether you will fight, because you almost certainly will. If you don't, someone is most assuredly repressing something—either that, or both of you are graduates of the DeVry Institute of Technology. No, the real experiment in this case is how sincerely she laughs when you tell all of your friends how comical it was when she fastened that wire with a widget instead of a thingumabob.

Another procedure I've found quite effective in assessing the mettle of your coupling is to spend an hour or two together in rush hour traffic on a ninety-five-degree day in an unair-conditioned car, preferably behind either a car that is burning oil or a truck hauling cooking fat for recycling. To improve on this even further, string four or five of these days together. For those of you in the snowbelt at a loss as to what to do alternatively in the winter months, I suggest getting caught in an unexpected snowstorm and then spending the next six hours of your hour-long commute dodging stalled cars, patches of ice, and spontaneous banks of snow. Again, for a stronger test, you may wish either to run out of gas or to lodge your car in a snow bank. My girlfriend and I have found you can up the ante even further by having been unprepared and so having no boots or gloves, all of which is even further exacerbated if you fiercely need to use a restroom.

On a different note, either one of you might also try experimenting with getting shigellosis or breaking a foot. It's amazing how something as tiny as a bacteria or as serendipitous as a semidebilitating accident can check the strength of your commitment. Shigellosis, for instance, increased our level of intimacy in ways we'd never imagined.... If your purpose, however, is to avoid a mess, this is definitely not the way to go.

Another traditional route in the community for probing the character of your relationship is going to the Michigan Womyn's Music Festival. It's possible that another festival could be substituted, but there's something special about hauling two hundred pounds of gear a couple of miles into the woods, trying to ascertain where it is your friends have camped, setting up your tent at night (or, better yet, at night in the pouring rain), and then sleeping, for the next three or four days, on hard, lumpy ground. It really cements a relationship together. Yeah, right!

If you're just moving in together and you want to get an early start on seeing how you are likely to fare as a couple, and you don't think moving and arranging furniture together is enough of a challenge, try bringing a cat with you into the relationship—preferably one that throws up a lot ("I didn't know vomit could *be* that shade of red"), scratches the furniture, or pees on valued articles of clothing, especially your lover's. If you're not a cat lover, a dog will do fine, particularly one who enjoys mud wrestling with skunks; who forgets, now and then, the fine distinctions between inside and outside the house; or who is passionately and romantically attracted to the shins of your lover and friends.

The truth is, of course, that there is no need whatsoever to go looking for ways in which to test your relationship: such tests will come along all on their own with unnerving regularity, like new revelations of Bill Clinton's infidelities, foibles, and major screw-ups. It is also true that not every adventure that life takes you on together provides mind-bending insights into your relationship. Nor should it, necessarily.

Take the adventure of house buying. While this process can be eye-opening about a lot of things—including your girlfriend's previously undisclosed fondness for faux knotty pine paneling and the fact that some people are perfectly comfortable living with buckets of minnows in their kitchen or a two-foot layer of clothing on the floor—it needn't shake up your relationship in any significant way. Sure it's stressful—in an exciting kind of way—but so is dating. And presumably, if you are searching for a house together, you and your gal have already done the dating thing together at least once or twice, so it's not like you don't have experience going through this sort of stressful thing with one another.

The process of house hunting is eerily similar to dating. First there's the search. Where lesbians seeking other lesbians might go to, say, a bar to check out the clientele, lesbians looking for houses go hang out at a realty office to ogle the property listings. You can't tell too much at this superficial level, in either case, but you can eliminate a few: this one looks too trendy for you and out of your reach, that one just isn't your style, and so on.

When you eventually spy one (house/woman) that causes your heart to skip a beat, you make a date. Naturally, you're a little nervous your first time. What kind of questions should you ask? Will this be the "right one"? How will you know? And of course, the odds are against turning up a perfect match right off the bat. You start again. And again. And again. Your friends are supportive and say things like, "Don't worry. The right one will come along." Or, "There's one out there for you somewhere. Just be patient." You begin to doubt the truth of these statements, but you force yourself to keep looking, to keep hanging out at the bar/realty company, getting chummy with the bartender/realtor. Occasionally, you do see a promising prospect but often, before you can even act, said prospect is scooped up by some lucky other. "All the good ones are taken," you mutter.

Discouraged, you vow to stop looking. "My life was pretty good before I started all this. I'm just making myself miserable." But you don't have the courage of your convictions. Besides, looking has become a habit, part of your routine.

After what seems like a lifetime (but you later realize was only a couple of months), suddenly, you are stricken by the plain not flashy one that was there all along which you were too distracted to even notice. This one, you decide, is growing cuter by the moment. You hate to be "looksist," but you can't help dreaming about those trim red bricks, that campy pink tub, those milky white appliances. Before you know it, you find yourself having made a thirty-year commitment—after a scant few hours of getting acquainted. How lesbian can you get?

Once the two of you have found the house of your dreams, the adventure isn't over. Funny things start to happen to you, when you own your own home. Becoming a homo-ner is like taking a mind-altering drug. Your first clue that something is different is that your family and coworkers begin to acknowledge your relationship—with the house. "How's the house?" they will ask, as if that were your primary relationship. What's really frightening is that you suspect it is.

Soon after, you discover your Marshall Field's credit card has fallen into disuse while your Sears card starts looking frayed around the edges. In fact, on a Sunday afternoon, when previously you might have lazed around the apartment or gone biking or taken in a movie, you find yourself wandering around Sears looking wistfully, longingly at power tools, shovels, screen doors, faucets, and garage door openers. You are on a first name basis with Ralph in the paint department.

You begin to notice changes in your lover/co-home-owner as well, like: when you asked her what she wanted for her birthday, she didn't say, "The new Melissa Etheridge CD." Or, "A new sweater." Or even, "A new baseball mitt or boots from L. L. Bean." No, instead, she asked for: "A wheelbarrow or a wet/dry vac." Though I tried to persuade Kathy that something, umm, more romantic might be in order, she insisted those aforementioned items were what she truly wanted. I finally broke down and bought her a red wheelbarrow. It was her favorite gift. And when there is the least little hint of warmth in the air, come spring, I become a landscape widow. She spends hours in the yard doing what we like to call "putzing around."

Another shocking change is that you begin to talk like your parents. No sooner have you signed your name one thousand and eight times at the closing than out of your mouth you hear coming phrases like, "Close the door please—you're letting the heat escape." Or, "If you're done in there, could you turn that light off?" Or, "Hey you kids—get out of the flower bed!" Worse still, I've found we have started to *act* like our parents. I, like my father before me, find I have begun to hate leaving The House. Departing from our humble abode, I experience the worst separation anxiety I've had since I was two, when Mom took away B, my beloved upchuck-stained bear, to be washed. Kathy, for her part, like any number of the hausfraus who populated the horizon of my Milwaukee youth, is engaged in a constant struggle to keep our urban yard in a pristine natural condition—which is no small task, considering the endless cycle of wrappers from the nearby Taco Bell and McDonald's tumbling across our lawn like mutant leaves and the neighborhood youngsters—those rascally Our Gang kids of the nineties—seeking to express themselves on our garage. We yearn for a simpler place—like Vermont, where if there are gangs at all, Kathy speculates the gang symbol of choice would be an upside-down cow.

In addition to waxing nostalgic about a more picket-fence time and place, we were surprised to discover a growing store of arcane knowledge between us. When you become a homeowner, you just *know* things. Like: garbage pickup is on Tuesdays. And: Marvin windows are the best. And: A. O. Smith makes top-of-the-line water heaters.

You also learn to put up with things you would *never*

let a landlord get away with. The drippy faucet in the kitchen we intend to fix someday is one thing, but we also lived for many, many months with linoleum in the upstairs hallway ripped off in patches, exposing glue-mottled wood flooring, while we awaited a time when we had the dough to get the floor refinished. There was also a period of several months when we fell asleep to the music of water pinging into a half-dozen receptacles artfully arranged about the bedroom before we could get the roof repaired.

Some other weird things start happening to you, too. You begin trading the names of contractors, like baseball cards, with your homeowner friends. You send holiday greetings to your plumber and carpenter. The thought of new appliances excites you a little more than you're comfortable with. You talk to people you normally wouldn't find yourself talking to—like the young burnout father of a growing brood next door, who sprinkles his conversations liberally with the word "man," as in, "Think about it, man," and who can't remember if you're Kathy—or Yvette.

What really gives me pause, though, when I stop to think about it, is just how easily Kath and I have slipped into this Ozzie and Harriet sort of existence. We have now even replaced my sporty little Honda CRX with a four-door "family car" and have been known to double date with Kathy's parents (*that* is truly scary). We would probably be members of the PTA, if we had children. People sometimes ask us if the neighbors give us any trouble about, you know, the lesbian thing. But I don't think that's how they perceive us. I think they see us *as just like them*—except that *we* don't drain our radiator fluid directly into the alley and don't douse our lawn with chemicals. If ever two people were made for the All-American monogamous lifestyle, it's us'ns. To make the picture complete, I am thinking of getting a bubble-pipe to puff on in my study—I already have the butch-looking plaid flannel slippers.

As it turns out, it's a good thing we're quite comfortable with our identity as a couple, because if we weren't, it would be highly disconcerting those times when I answer the phone and my mother-in-law greets me, "Hi, Kath." *Many* people, actually, cannot tell us apart on the phone and claim that we have begun to sound alike. Better that than they shouldn't be able to tell which of us they are speaking to in person. Which happens with some frequency in lesbian couples. Surely you've had occasion to notice how similar two women can look after they've been together for several years. Of course, that's not much of a mystery when you consider that, by and large, we all buy our clothes at The Gap and we all had pretty much the same haircut for years—either the clean-cut boy of the early sixties look or, among the femme wannabes, the long hair in the back, short on the sides style, which was, speaking hair historically, invented by Paul Revere and the Raiders, I think.

That Kath and I can apparently no longer lay claim to our own distinctive voices is not nearly as alarming to me as the certitude that we now even seem to share the same brain. Frequently, it is not even necessary for either of us to finish a sentence because the other one will do it for her. This is a good development for me, though, as, often by the time I get midway through a sentence I myself have long since forgotten how I intended to end it. More unnerving still is that, probably as a consequence of the one brain thing, we appear gradually to be developing our own language—kind of like that weird twin thing. We could compose a rather long list of abbreviations, code words, and alternative usages that have become a regular part of our conversational patterns when alone together. An offshoot of this, perhaps, is our spontaneous generation of totally nonsensical pet names for one another, like cheese weasel and babyhead and a hundred others I still have enough sense not to share lest I be suspected of a psychotic break. What I fear is that one day I will no longer have that good sense and will say to Kath in public, "Hey, Weenie Popeil, do you have any cc's? Some wimbliness is occurring." But all lesbian couples are like this, right?

Anyway, having firmly established that Kath and I are indeed the marrying kind, I find myself wondering how it is I should refer to her who is the light of my life—in language understood by someone besides the two of us, that is. Normally, we lesbos are right there on the cutting edge with language, but in the area of giving expression to our relationship with the one special woman in our life, we have fallen down on the job. Though the existing terms from which we have to choose are reasonably diverse, none of them seems quite right overall. Here's what I mean:

Roommate. This is appropriate to use only in the most desperate of situations: when you're in the closet, for instance, and are introducing "her" to your mom, your boss, or the priest at your sister's wedding. Otherwise, it sounds like all you share is a love for tacking posters on your wall and a jar of peanut butter.

Friend. Although this implies more of the intimacy that characterizes your relationship than does "roommate," and while certainly one would hope being friends is at least part of your relationship, it is still only describing *part* of your relationship. "Friend" puts her on about the same level as Lynn Fliss, the girl you used to jump rope with in third grade. Is this really how you want people to see you as a couple? Of course, adding the word "special" to "friend" gives it a nudge-nudge wink-wink sort of quality, but it still seems less than satisfactory to me.

Girlfriend. While this gets at the actual basis of the relationship in a high school sort of way ("Kath and I are going steady") and is knowledgeably and commonly used among ourselves, it reminds me of something my grandmother would say—meaning something altogether different, as in "Your sister was here with her girlfriend Pam." (Oh really. Does Lori's *husband* know about this?) Then there's the issue of the derogatoriness of the word "girl" when used to refer to an adult of the female gender. But what's the alternative—"woman friend"? Definitely a phrase of the blue-haired lady set. And we're not talking punk here.

Wife. Oh sure, many of us have joked about wanting our own Alice B. Toklas to cook and clean for us and to assure us that we're geniuses, but frankly, picturing Kath in a housedress and apron is not an image I cherish. There is an alternative here, of course: "husband." But if I wanted someone to sit around the house all day Saturday wearing sweats, watching TV, and scratching, I'd do it myself.

Significant other. This sounds like something right out of a Soc. 101 textbook. While it does have the advantage of being gender nonspecific, few of us ever use it without a wry edge to our voices. And no wonder: it's so darn clinical. Most of us have cherished therapists, but who wants them naming our relationships? I mean, do you let your vet name your cats?

Sweetie, honey, and other aspartame epithets. Even the most macho among us have our mushy moments, but when you subject others to such pet names, you risk making them gag or plunging them into a diabetic coma. Yes, we want to take our lifestyle "out of the closet and into the streets," but some things are just *too* private to be shared—like introductions beginning, "This is my widdle snuggle bunny. . . ."

Old lady. I don't know where to begin talking about what's wrong with this one. So I won't.

Love of my life. Too long. And besides, just how many new women can you introduce like that before being laughed out of the room by your friends? (Honest, honey, I've never said that about anyone but you.)

Partner. Unlike wife, this indicates an egalitarian relationship—maybe too equal, like a business associate or a fellow bridge player. I've tried amplifying this term when describing our relationship on legal-type documents by saying "domestic partner," but for some reason this makes me think of cows on a farm more than, say, a lesbian couple.

Lover. Though probably the best of the lot, this term has a certain illicit quality about it (wives and fiancées vs. mistresses and lovers) and implies *only* a sexual relationship. If those studies on long-term lesbian relationships are correct, this word is probably a misnomer for most of us. . . .

So now that I've effectively eliminated every option we currently have, what's left? Well, it just so happens that I have found the perfect term in Mary Daly's *Wickedary:* "boon companion," which she defines as "an intimate friend . . . a companionate blessing." Okay, I'll admit it seems a little strange on the tongue at first, but trust me: it kinda grows on you. It's so warm and *homey*. Go ahead—try it a few times. If we all use it, it's bound to catch on. "Mom, Dad. This is my boon companion, Estelle. We're thinking of buying a house together. . . ."

Who Holds The Purse Strings When No One Owns A Purse?

The category is: Most Likely to Cause Trouble in a Lesbian Relationship. And the winner is—oops, there's a three-way tie: sex, housecleaning, and money. Not that any of these things are guaranteed to be unproblematic for any relationship, but they are particularly complicated for lesbians because, unlike hetero couples, lesbian couples can't fall back on the time-worn guidelines for human behavior in these areas: we'll do it whenever *I* want to, *you'll* do it, and I don't care if your salary *is* larger than mine—my thing is bigger than yours, so I'm in charge. Every aspect of lesbian existence is made more troublesome by the fact that neither party of the couple possesses the baton of power. Decisions of how to "do" money are no exception.

Sitcoms and comedians through the ages have made it clear that male-female couples have their share of relational strife over financial differences—usually because the wife has a tendency to go out recklessly brandishing a charge card. Even before little rectangles of plastic came into vogue as a way to dispose of one's income quickly and efficiently, women like Lucy, with the help of her "best friend" Ethel (nudge, nudge, wink, wink), were able to discover ways to fritter away Ricky's hard-earned bongo-playing money while fulfilling their lust for goofy-looking hats and the latest Paris fashions. Women have always been resourceful, it seems.

In spite of these tiffs over money management within the hetero couple of our parents' generation, there was a commonly recognized method for the handling of incoming resources. Marriage vows—"Do you promise to love, honor, and open a joint checking account?"—made it pretty much a fait accompli that the couple would pool their resources. Back then, of course, the husband's resources generally consisted of dough, as in money, while the wife's consisted of dough, as in lumpy loaves of bread. In many hetero couples today, however, both people are working, and as a consequence, it is no longer necessarily the case that money all gets thrown into the same pot. Nevertheless, it is still *possible* to fall back on the Ricardo model of household economics, and many hetero households do. Unless, that is, one of them is rich and makes the other sign a prenuptial agreement. Lesbians—barring Martina—historically have not been faced with the dilemma of having gobs of money they needed to safeguard against gold-digging little butches. Because of this and because no one wears the pants in the family in lesbian households or because both people do or because they alternate pants-wearing on odd-even butch-femme days, it all gets terribly confusing as to who's handling the money and how. This is not to say that gays and lesbians aren't as familiar with the Ricardo model as anyone else—hey, we not only have TVs but most of us have heterosexual parents as well. It's just that this method has no more of a long-standing tradition than any other for same sex couples. Now if we had been watching Ricky and Fred set up housekeeping together—or better yet, Lucy and Ethel—it might be a different story. As it is, we are pretty much on our own when it comes to monitoring the comings and goings of money.

Basically, here's how *we* do it in our house: put all of our money into our joint checking account and spend it till it's gone—and apparently, the faster the better. Actually, when my lover and I started out, in an attempt to maintain some façade of independence, we kept our individual checking accounts on life support systems even as we opened the monolithic and ever frightening *joint account*—which, as lesbians, is about as near as we get to declaring our engagement. Anyway, this account, we said, was for household expenses—rent, gas, electricity, Ben and Jerry's, toilet paper, bubble bath, more Ben and Jerry's. Our individual accounts were for personal expenses, although frankly, I don't see how much more personal you can get than *toilet* paper. We were rather proud of this system, ignoring, for the first couple of months, the fact that by the end of each month one or the other of us would run out of money in her individual account and have to "borrow" money from the other. Eventually, though, it became apparent even to us—as debts were forgiven or forgotten or had grown as unwieldy as the national one—that the lines between "hers" and "mine" had grown awfully fuzzy. But we still hung on to this system as a fair, equitable, and totally noncodependent way to handle our finances.

As monthly finance charges began to mount and as we valiantly tried to keep *three* checkbooks balanced, it occurred to me that it was foolish to maintain this limp symbol of independence when the symbol was so clearly—and literally—an empty one: I ditched my individual checking account. A month or two later, wouldn't you know it, but the same darn thing occurred to Kathy. Actually, what it amounted to was we both had finally given up any pretense of being economically independent. Thus reads the account of our heroic but losing struggle against the weight of our puny salaries and inadequate budgeting skills.

At least I think our budgeting skills were lousy. Let me just ask you this: Did *you* go out and buy a VCR when one of you was unemployed?

That's what I thought.

To say Kathy and I *chose* our joint financial path would be something of an overstatement—a little like saying Reagan was "aware" of exactly what was going on during the Iran Contra thing. But it did give us a feeling of being in control, not unlike the King in *The Little Prince* ordering the sun to rise every morning. I am not recommending this as a course of action for everyone and anyone. It takes a special sense of trust—and ineptitude—to set up a system of finances in the way we did. In fact, I know of a number of couples who have diverged from our carefully laid out financial plan.

One couple I know has a sophisticated system in

which the receipts from every household purchase—annotated with the purchaser's name—are put into a jar and added up at the end of the month. If one partner has paid out more money, the other repays her for half the sum of the difference. Kath and I remain in awe of the sheer mathematicalness of this system. Knowing us, we would be stymied almost immediately by not being able to decide which jar to use. I would want to go out and purchase a receptacle dedicated to that purpose—a tasteful decanter, for instance—while Kath would more likely suggest something practical, like washing out the emptied wheat germ jar.

Other couples we know routinely split every joint purchase or expense right down the middle. This seems straightforward enough but requires more vigilance than Kathy and I can seem to muster: What if one of us uses more tampons out of the box? Do we take the price of the box and divide by twenty-two to determine a per tampon rate? And then there's the differential moisturizer use. We would have to install a meter on the lotion bottle's pump and determine a per push rate. I can see the smoke rising from the calculator's overheated little keys, not to mention from my brain, at the simple thought of these high-level financial dealings.

Still others, influenced, perhaps, by years of toting out the euphemism "this is my roommate," continue to retain a hers-and-hers attitude about purchases, each paying half of the rent and such but steadfastly cordoning off her own books, chairs, band-aids, and cheese curls. This takes way too much mental effort for me. If I can't even remember today's date or when I got this pimply thing on my tongue, how is it that I will remember who bought that Madonna CD four years ago? A Dynamo label-maker could come in handy here, I guess, but do I really want such incontrovertible proof that it was me who had the bad taste to acquire *Wayne's World* on video?

The prize for the most PC financial arrangement goes to a couple that Kathy knows who divides up household expenses *proportionally*. That is, each of them pays a percentage of each item based on her salary relative to that of her partner. This agreement seems fine if one of you is some sort of idiot savant with numbers, like that guy in *Rain Man,* but for us regular people—people who improved their math skills by learning to score bowling—you might as well ask us to explain the theory of relativity.

In all honesty, though, I have to say that while our method—laziness—works for us, throwing all your money into a joint checking account is not without its problems. First of all, there's the decision of whose name goes first on the checks. We went with alphabetical, although, as someone who's initials are YZ, I have to say that I'm not entirely sure I see the equity of this solution. . . . Having once settled that issue, though, there are more: What kind of checks do you get—the plain pinstriped kind, which you want, or the ones with a different Simpson on each one, which she wants? Who gets to carry the checkbook? And how do you send away for a gift for your girlfriend without her knowing about it?

If you have scads of money, this last might not be a problem: just take out cash under the pretext of "mad" money and get a money order. In a household like ours, where each of us knows where every penny is at any given moment and what it was spent on, a big ol' withdrawal is bound to be noticed. Ours is not the kind of household where you are even likely to find spare change in the couch cushions. Popcorn, maybe. But dimes or nickels—no.

I myself was faced with this particular joint checking account problem not more than a couple of years ago. In order to buy my baby the compost bin of her dreams for her birthday ("What a shitty little present," as our friend Laura said), I took out a loan from my credit union at work and gave the cash thus acquired to a friend, who then wrote a check to the compost people. This plan worked like a charm: Kathy never suspected a thing.

Still, *the* biggest issue when two folks opt to pool their money is what, of all the thousands and millions of things there are to buy, to spend that money on. Lesbian ex-nuns probably don't have a problem with the temptations presented by Gap Wear and Starbuck's coffee and Doc Martens shoes and Jeep Cherokees. They're used to a spartan existence. Then again, what do I know? Maybe they left nunhood *because* they wanted these things. What I can tell you is that money has a tendency to leave *our* little fingers like yolk out of a cracked egg.

As a consequence, we have come up with a good cop–bad cop strategy for dealing with impulse buying, theoretically alternating roles as to who will be the grown-up on any given occasion and say, "We cannot buy this five-cubic-foot freezer today." Unfortunately, most days we could really use a third cop, with both of us all too often unable to muster up any meanness of spirit. I, in particular, am bad at it, and have a tendency to burst into tears the minute a pout even thinks about appearing on Kathy's lovely lips. Where was the bad cop, for instance, the day we bought that rototiller? Or my Sorel boots? Or the laptop computer?

The truth is, we love shopping together—kiwis and mangos, aerobics videos, broken bags of topsoil, major appliances, books, doohickies to hang our toothbrushes on: it really doesn't matter what we shop for, as long as we're together, buying things we really *need.* I suspect this is not healthy. And frankly, I'm not quite sure why we so enjoy shopping together, given our totally different shopping styles: I like to browse, while Kathy can tell if there is any apparel to her liking simply by crossing the threshold into the store. Much to the detriment of our checking account, though, we seem to have overcome this basic incompatibility well enough to have had our Visa card limit raised about once a year every year since we've been together.

Actually, Kathy has turned into a financial whiz. She now reads the business section of the paper on a semiregular basis and is de facto in charge of all our financing and refinancing and retirement accounts and investments and wherever else our money goes besides into things that end up hanging in my closet. I, on the other hand, have never progressed beyond the balancing-the-checkbook/paying-the-bills stage. "I feel like such a *wife,*" I recently confided to a friend. This may not have been the best choice of words given that this friend actually *is* a wife, in the traditional sense. However, being the good friend she is, she did not comment on my sarcastic use of a title she had claimed as her own. Instead, she tried to reassure me that my interests just don't lie in the financial direction. She's probably right.

Still, I have this vision of me sitting at home forty years from now, my hair faintly blue, wondering what a mutual fund is and if it has anything to do with Jim tagging wild animals in Africa while his white-haired friend talks about insurance. Not only that, but I'm not sure I'll be able to reprogram the thermostat either. Sad to say, but I think Kathy is enabling my duh-ness.

Even so, sometimes I have to wonder if I've put myself in the right hands. Kathy's latest plan to cement our financial success is for both of us to quit our jobs, cash in our retirement accounts, and use it all to buy lotto tickets. The worst part is, some days I find myself thinking about the efficacy of this plan. It's a good thing we don't have any dependents relying on us for an inheritance. . . .

Which One Of You Is The Mother?

It used to be from time to time you would hear of women who said when they got married they knew they were attracted to women but they wanted children. Well, now that science has made it possible for lesbians to have babies by themselves, there's *no* reason to get married—unless, of course, you happen to prefer people with a whole lot more hair on their backs and bellies than most of the lesbians I know.

The maternal instinct tends to be strong among women, lesbian or otherwise, although it's hard to say how much of that is nature, how much nurture. In my family, four out of five grandmothers surveyed preferred baby dolls as the gift of choice for prepubescent girls. I didn't stand a fighting chance with those odds, but fight I did anyway. Instead of dolls, I lobbied mightily for a bicycle, shoes with springs on the bottom, stilts, a pogo stick, books of any sort, and lizards. If a spring-loaded baby doll or one on wheels I could ride had been available, I might have been more interested in acquiring one. As it was, those little hunks of plastic molded to look like human infants offered no transportation options whatsoever—and, apparently, judging from the list of items I most coveted, I was looking for an escape vehicle. Either that, or I was practicing for a shot at joining the Ringling Brothers Barnum and Bailey circus later in life.

Or maybe my disinterest in dolls was the result of the fact that I had met the real thing already, in the form of my baby sister, and I wasn't too thrilled with it. As a toddler this cherubic little red-faced thing had bitten me in the butt—*through my pajamas*—and drawn blood. I saw no reason to get another of those for my very own, thereby risking more puncture wounds.

Even I, with my unnatural preference for unusual forms of locomotion over plastic replicas of human infants, even I was haunted by the ghost of uteri past. My grandmother tells me that, in my teen years, I declared to her in no uncertain terms that I wanted children someday—though not necessarily a husband to go with them. I must have been prescient on two counts, because *(1)* I didn't even know I was a lesbian yet, and *(2)* at the time, if the technology for such a virgin birth existed, the general public was certainly not aware of it—except for the one time in Bethlehem, of course, and I don't think anyone was really expecting a repeat performance of that event any time soon, and certainly not from little heathen moi.

Fortunately, the urge to produce little carbon copies

of myself passed—only to resurface again, when both my lesbian tendencies and the technology for test tube babies and such had been firmly established. With the advent of artificial insemination, suddenly the question "Do you want children someday?" began coming up on second or third dates. And I was usually the one asking it. I bought all the books on lesbian moms available at the time (all two of them), spent hours daydreaming about baby names (Andy or Mickey, if it was a girl, something less butch, if it was a boy), and tried to imagine a sack of Idaho potatoes passing through that tiny, tiny space. Then I would go into remission from babyitis for a year or two at a time and live my life normally, as though I were not harboring this grave affliction.

I thought I was completely cured when Kathy entered my life. I persisted in thinking this even though, as Kathy pointed out, if a baby, any baby, was anywhere within my line of sight—forget about trying to hold a coherent conversation with me. Kathy, however, was experiencing no such state of denial: it was clear to both of us she was suffering from a full-blown case of I-want-a-babyism. Living in close proximity to one another as the two of us do, it was hard not to come down with it again myself.

Okay, we said, on what might have been about our tenth or twelfth date if we hadn't actually been living together by then, let's have a baby in five years. It seemed like such a good time frame, in fact, that we said the same thing several years later: let's have a baby in five years. The birth of our child was *always* five years away. But that's okay: we needed the time to pick out names (which we couldn't agree on), to decide about religious upbringing (which we couldn't agree on), and to figure out who would have the kid (Kathy). Eventually, after years of waiting until we were more financially solvent, I put it to Kath this way: "Either we can go out to dinner and see a movie once in awhile, or, we can have a kid." It had become evident to us, with our nonprofit jobs, that we would never have enough money to do both. We opted for a social life and for avoiding filing for Chapter 13.

We decided, instead, to become really good at the aunt thing. And that's just fine and dandy with me. I have never felt a particular need to experience the miracle of something trying to kickbox its way out of my abdomen and attach itself like a leech to my chest. Maybe my biological clock has run down or maybe it's digital and I just don't hear it ticking, but I have reached a time in my life when cradling someone else's baby and kissing its fuzzy little head is enough of a maternal rush for me. Now if our siblings would only oblige us and give us some material to work with as aunts, we'd be set.

And Kath and I have not been alone in our delusions of future motherhood. One of our friends was so convinced she would have children someday that she had been stockpiling baby clothes for years. Having since reached a conclusion not unlike our own, she now has a rather large stash of baby shower presents—which, as it turns out in our community, will definitely come in handy: I, along with Kathy, have hosted two of these showers and have been to at least a couple more.

Actually, go to *any* lesbian function, and babies, if not a physical presence, will be present in at least one or more of the conversations. Pictures will be shown, amazing achievements discussed ("she rolled over!"), methods of gettin' 'em debated, and solutions to parenting woes shared. You would think lesbians had just discovered this thing called motherhood. And in a way we have.

It just slays me to hear, on those talk shows and in court rooms, that lesbians shouldn't be allowed to raise children. It kills me because, honey, no other child could be more planned for or wanted as the child of lesbians. It's not like we're having these kids by accident! "Oh, damn, honey—I forgot to take my birth control pill. How 'bout you?" And it's not even like artificial insemination can be done on a whim: "Hey, hon, you know what might be fun today? What do you say you and I go find some guy, have him tested for AIDS, and then get a thimble of his sperm and put it inside you and see what happens. Doesn't that sound like a kick? Let's hop on the Harley and go." And to my way of thinking, although this is not something you might want to argue in a court of law, lesbians certainly couldn't do much worse than a lot of our parents did! And speaking of courts of law, one of the ironies of our time is that courts have been known to take babies away from lesbian moms—on the premise that the child might turn out to be a lesbian—and turn the kids over to the mom's mother, a woman who has *already* raised at least one lesbian. Now there's logic for you.

Anyway, all I can say is, it's a good thing Kathy and I opted to forgo the motherhood thing. Not because we wouldn't make good parents, mind you, but because we would have had trouble deciding among the various means of acquiring said children. We can hardly decide what *restaurant* to go to of an evening, much less decide among adoption, artificial insemination, and the old-fashioned way, in which, of course, you *earn* that baby. Truthfully, though, I think in our case at least, we could pretty much eliminate this last. As if all of *that* weren't enough to decide, there are nuances to each option that must be considered as well.

Like with artificial insemination—are you going to go with fresh? Or frozen? And is this question any easier if you pretend like you're just talking about peas? Should the donor be anonymous through a clinic or someone you know and, ergo, someone your child will eventually know? That's a tough one because, to be honest, there aren't all that many people with whom I would feel comfortable sharing the mysteries of my ovulation cycle. I also think it takes a very special kind of person to adhere to social conventions such as polite conversation and not gagging in public while someone is placing a warm container of his semen in your hand. But maybe I'm just socially inept. Really, there's no reason in the world why you wouldn't want to shake that man's hand in gratitude after he's so generously donated his little tail-wagging boys.

Adoption, of course, is no picnic either. Although things have slowly started to change, chances are that for many adoption agencies it will be necessary to cover up all traces of your lesbianism. This feat may require a fresh eye, as in all likelihood you will have long since lost any perspective on the dead-giveaway dyke aspects of your life. Is it a problem, for instance, that both of your names are on every legal document you've signed in the last however-many years? Will anyone be tipped off by the bin of sporting goods—football, baseball mitt, cleats, volleyball, tennis racket, and basketball—next to the Nautilus machine with the poster of Martina beside it for inspiration? Do you even know, anymore, when you're calling her "baby"? This last probably won't be a problem, though, in that you may have had to move into separate living quarters for the duration of the adoption proceedings—a prospect that is not exactly conducive to the kind of intimacy one normally thinks of as preceding the having of children.

And it *is* ever so romantic, I've heard, kneeling beside your beloved, holding an eye dropper of some guy's jizz over her vagina, while she screams at you, "Come on—just do it, would you? I'm getting cold here." Sure, at first, there is a certain mystique about the process: here you are, the two of you, about to discover the miracle of life together, about to cement the bond between you even further with this shared experience. But when you (meaning the two of you) don't get pregnant the first time out like the nuns told you you would, and you're making your umpteenth run to the airport at midnight for that shipment of frozen semen from the out-of-state sperm bank, and calling all over town for dry ice to keep it on until *just* the right time in your cycle, or when you're putting egg whites in your vagina so the little guys can swim better and, consequently, smell like the breakfast plate from the local diner for the next several days—well, you can see just how romantic that would be. As some friends of ours once said, eventually you're just happy if you can keep the dog out of the bedroom and find the remote control.

Pregnancy itself is also terribly romantic. The image we have from TV is of an adoring couple sharing the feel of baby's first movements as she grows in the womb, the ultrasound pictures, and the sense of purpose and loving partnership in Lamaze classes. Well, I'm sure all of that happens in lesbian relationships too, but the part they mostly leave out are the mood swings and the awkward moments with the neighbors: "Oh, I didn't know you were married!" One of our friends was so emotional when she was pregnant that, when her girlfriend mentioned possibly dyeing her hair, she burst into tears and wailed, "But I *love* your gray hairs." And surprisingly enough, they were the only two lesbians in their suburban Lamaze class. So when it came time for the actual birth, which they planned to do at home, we wanted to be extra helpful and offered to rip up newspapers to put on the floor. Hey—we are nothing if not supportive. As it turned out, they ended up having to have a C-section, so our services were not called upon.

Though babies are not without their own challenges, the fun really begins when they get verbal. Children do not have quite the same boundaries we do. This is why our friends lived in fear the summer their daughter learned about her biological heritage: they had visions of her asking the other kids in the neighborhood who *their* "sperm daddies" were. Little kids, for the most part, see absolutely nothing wrong with having two moms—one seven-year-old I knew thought he was very lucky to have two moms when most kids only got one—and so will tell almost anyone this fact about themselves. Another little boy told a neighbor kid about his situation. "Now let me get this right," the kid responded. "You have two moms, no dad, and a dog? Cool."

Not everyone, of course, is so accepting of this news. Recently, our friends' daughter, age four, was talking to me on the phone, telling me about her new preschool. "My teacher Mrs. Bone didn't know I had two mommies," she said. "That must have been a surprise for her," I responded conversationally.

"Oh, she wasn't listening to me," she said. Aw: her first experience of denial.

Most of the time, of course, being a lesbian mom is just like being any other kind of mom. And their kids are just like any other kids. That's why, our friends tell us, they plan to enjoy their little urchins now. Because they fully expect that when the kids become teenagers they will hate them and threaten to run away to our house.

If, in spite of having read thus far, you still think you want to have kids, but aren't sure you're ready yet, you've come to the right place. I have compiled, for your benefit, a checklist of how you will know whether you are, in fact, prepared to enter . . . the baby twilight zone.

You are truly in tune with those baby vibes when. . .

1. You have begun to think clean clothing is overrated. This is a good first step: babies and small children are capable of cleverly concealing amazing quantities of food remnants, dirt, and other less pleasant substances on their persons in any number of places. When you least expect it, they produce artful displays of these items on anything from your most torn and faded t-shirt to your snazziest dry-clean-only silk blouse. Babies don't discriminate.

2. It does not matter to you that your friends won't socialize with you because you have a baby. Infants and toddlers introduce a certain, shall we say, spontaneity to any conversation or social gathering. This may be difficult for your, um, goal-oriented friends to deal with. It will come to your attention that some of these friends—not wanting to make you feel bad by inviting you to an event that you *certainly* couldn't come to anyway because of the baby—will simply stop inviting you.

3. It doesn't matter that your friends *only* want to socialize with you because you have a baby. For every one of your antibaby friends, there will be friends who are lesbian-mom wannabes, who discover they are much more interested in your children than they ever were in you. Or at least that's the way it seems to you. Also, you will find yourself with brand new friends, friends with whom the only thing you may have in common is that they, too, are lesbian moms.

4. You think sleep deprivation might be a fun thing to try. Babies are like evil little preverbal psychologists: part of their raison d'être is to see how you will function with disrupted sleep patterns. If this is your idea of a good time, you are definitely ready for parenthood.

5. You have begun to regret not being the center of attention at any restaurant where you dine. People are unfriendly in twentieth-century urban America, you say? Put a baby on your lap or at your table, and people react as though you had put up a flashing neon sign saying, "Come talk to me. I really didn't want to eat anyway, just because my food is sitting here getting cold. . . ." A baby is a secret entry into a world of instant intimacy with total strangers. They will ask you questions such as, "How old is he?" referring to your beautiful bib-overall-clad daughter. Or "Which one of you is the mother?" while looking back and forth, in a confused fashion, between your lover and yourself. Encouraged by your forthcomingness, often they will proceed to tell you, in great detail, of the little ones in their own lives. In the meantime, your own darling angel, bored by all this conversation, will proceed to arch her back and scream—guaranteeing you even more attention.

6. You feel the need for more unsolicited advice in your life. This is good. Because you will find that just about everyone knows how to take better care of your baby than you do, and they will offer advice freely, without your even having to ask! In fact, total strangers will feel they know your baby *so* well that they can speak for him. "Mommy, I'm so cold. Please cover me up better with that blanket."

7. Short excursions just haven't seemed challenging enough lately. Having a baby will definitely alleviate this problem in your life. Aside from all of the stuff you will need to pack, even for a trip to the grocery store sometimes, there is the challenge of getting the kid in the car safely and securely. Babies think of car seats as infant prisons and can suddenly develop several extra limbs and superhuman strength when you try to lock 'em into one of those things.

8. You are looking for a good excuse never to read a book again. Every mom I know, at least for the first several years of the child's life, all but gave up on reading anything more involved than the instructions for making Gerber oatmeal or a page, now and then, from something like *Breastfeeding Your Toddler.* Babies, like cats, are anti-intellectual and can always think of something else for you to do.

9. You have been feeling that sex is overrated and you've spent way too much time on it. Adding a baby to your life is the perfect way to remedy that. Between being totally exhausted (that sleep deprivation thing) and always tuned to the baby-cry wavelength, you will rarely be in the right frame of mind for sex. Also, any number of tiny tots refuse to sleep anywhere else but with you, the center of their existence. While this outright adoration and chronic cuddliness is not without its rewards, one of them is not making a sacrosanct space in your life for adult passion.

10. You have been running out of things to talk about lately. Women with babies always have a story to tell. You might find, however, that others are not *nearly* so riveted by the details of the color and consistency of what you find in baby's diapers as you are and that they don't find half as hysterical as you do the fact that, while you were playing with the little booboo, raising her up and down over your head, she let loose a glob of spit-up right into your open mouth. But this is how you separate the wheat from the chaff: your true, true friends, the ones who really love you, will be just as fascinated by your offspring as you are.

Now as you know, I myself am not a mother (and I don't even play one on TV), but believe these things I'm telling you: they're all true. I have it on the best of authority.

Babies, it's true, have certain charms that can override myriad doubts and concerns—all the more reason, if you are the least bit susceptible to those charms, to be sure you are as prepared as possible before you plunge in. So photocopy this list and tack it up on your fridge as a reminder of what all is involved. Because babies, like swimsuits, are nonreturnable.

How To Spell Lover With An X

Among the many things in life I hope I never have to go through again—along with adolescence, surgery, and watching another episode of "Three's Company"—is the breakup of a relationship. Because, as it turns out, Neil Sedaka was absolutely right: breaking up *is* hard to do. Your average lesbian, during her heyday, can break up as many as two or three times *per year*—sometimes with the same person. If it's so damn hard, why do we do it so much? Other than the sheer pleasure, I'd have to say the main reason is that a lesbian is likely to share a mailbox with you long before she shares the fact that, for instance, she has not quite gotten over her last lover or that she has a deep-seated biological need never to see a dish sitting idly in the sink.

It is a long-established truism that the finer shades of

the word "dating" elude most lesbians. We don't date—we mate. After two dinners, a night out dancing, one foray into the world of l'amour, and an outing to meet "the friends"—voilà: you are now part of a couple. As a consequence, you can no longer just stop dating this other woman: you have to break up with her. Ex-lovers can be acquired quite rapidly in this way.

I myself have had my share of . . . unusual . . . relationships for precisely these reasons. Thanks to a friend of mine—who adores hearing the stories, over and over again, of how wacky either my exes were or my relationship with each of them was—the entertainment value of my past amorous encounters does not escape me. This friend has actually suggested I write a *book* about my ex-lovers. Flattered as I was by this proposal to detail for the entire world what a fool I have been, I am not in the kind of tax bracket yet that would give me the financial leeway to hire a bodyguard. So, for now, I think it's best if I steer clear of the particulars of my past relationships. I don't want to end up with a lawsuit for slander or an unexpected ride in an ambulance.

Also preventing me from doing a kiss-and-tell sort of book is karma: the possibility that someone will write a hefty tome about *my* foibles. If I had no other reasons, this alone would make me loath to split up with Kathy. For while the aforementioned exes would no doubt not be averse to waxing rhapsodic about some of my "virtues," none of them know me quite so well as my beloved Kathleen, with whom I have been involved since the late *eighties*. Oh, what a book she could write! What saves me from sheer terror is the knowledge that such a book wouldn't exactly make the best-seller list. Not like poor Martina, who, if things keep going the way they have been, may one day be the subject of an entire *series* authored by ex-girlfriends.

Most of us don't have to worry about that kind of notoriety, of course, but it's still a trifle unnerving to reflect on how, in an intimate relationship, among the many intimacies you share are juicy tidbits about *past* relationships. This is especially frightening when you consider the interconnectedness of the lesbian community. The interconnections among dykes in Chicago alone, if put on paper, would make a full human arterial map look like a simple geometric figure. Let me illustrate what I mean.

It's like this: you're talking to someone, X, whom you met at a social function to which you were invited by A, to whom you were originally introduced by a mutual acquaintance, B, and you discover that X's ex-lover once dated the ex-lover, C, of both B and B's ex, who is the roommate of the lover of A, who is an ex-lover of C's, and that X is a friend of someone you met through your ex-lover, who you met through the lover, D, of your friend E, and that X's lover once dated the ex-lover of the ex-lover of D. Follow me? No? Good. Neither do I. That's *exactly* what I mean by interconnections. When you further consider that, years ago, a number of women on the south side of Chicago put together a family tree, as it were, and discovered their roots went "all the way back" to Billie Jean King, the possibility of all these people knowing the particulars of your intimate relationship with someone somewhere in that chain becomes humbling, to say the least. I don't mean to imply that lesbians are indiscreet, but this phenomenon does make for an interesting potluck dinner.

Further complicating the whole ex-lover thing is the fact that it is not at all uncommon for lesbians to remain friends with someone with whom they are otherwise incompatible. In the beginning, it takes a while to figure out just how to relate to one another in this new way. An illustration of this uncertainty is gift-giving at birthdays and Christmas and such. If you just broke up with someone, you don't want to get her more than she's getting you because you don't want her to think you're still hung up on her, but you want to get her something nice so she won't think you're bitter. What makes this especially tricky is that you *are* still hung up on her *and* more than a little bitter. If one of you has started dating someone else, finding the right balance is an even more intricate process, as the new girlfriend is likely to be somewhat touchy about fond gestures between you and the woman with whom you were oh-so-recently snuggling naked.

Eventually, though, it's possible to settle into a comfortable friend/ex-lover relationship, which seems perfectly normal in a lesbian context. To put it in a hetero context, this would be like, say, my dad going on vacation with my mom and my stepfather. People might find this strange. But in the lesbian community, ex-lovers not only vacation with one another but also own businesses together, buy duplex houses jointly, and smooch—imagine the hilarity that ensues when the new lover's friends witness such sororial affection.

This is not to say that every relationship ends so amicably. The expression "dyke drama" does not refer to our remarkable thespian endeavors, after all. We're not talking *Philadelphia Story* Katherine Hepburn–Cary Grant type venom either: "Why Susan, dahling, you never could hold your tongue, could you dear?" "Don' be ridiculuth, Emiwy deah: I'm hoding it wight now." In my experience, lesbian anger doesn't tend to run toward the spirited exchange of witty barbs. Generally, a lesbian whom you have pissed off with your wayward ways is likely to respond in a more earthy fashion. Like letting the air out of your tires. Or energetically pointing out your faults to you and all your fellow party-goers. Or moving in with your best friend. Or coming out to your boss for you.

No matter what terms your relationship ends on, it can be rough getting through the period just following the termination of an amorous relationship. Now, at this point in my life, it seems pretty clear to me that I *can* get through it—having done so a number of times already. Consequently, any breakup drama that may have thrilled me in a perverse sort of way in the beginning—How will I ever survive this?—has disappeared and I just want to get the whole angst thing over with as quickly as possible. So, during my revolving door days, I amassed a variety of creative ways of surviving the break up. These methods include:

Buy a motor scooter. Or any other overly expensive, frivolous item you might be desiring. It's a way of saying, "I am a good person and I deserve wonderful things." Of course, when you've just been dumped, it may be difficult to actually believe this. But here's the beauty of buying something like a motor scooter—or VCR, TV, stereo, etc.: if you've just spent hundreds of dollars on yourself, you *must* be a wonderful person. Granted, you might not be feeling nearly so wonderful when those bills start arriving—but at least your dejection won't be because of the break up!

Let the house go to hell. A little self-indulgence. You can say to yourself, "I feel bad enough already without having to worry about bathtub ring and dull floors—besides, who's going to see it anyway?" This serves two purposes: *(1)* it gives you a chance to wallow in your own misery, if you feel so inclined, and *(2)* it gives you time to pursue other creative ways to pass the time. After a while, though—the length of time varies depending on the heinousness of the split—watching dust bunnies frolicking with the tumbleweeds of cat hair can get counterproductive and the squalor gets depressing. When that happens, it's time to:

Clean the house as if Melissa Etheridge were coming to visit. If you're in the right mood, this can be a great experience. Honest. Cleaning the house can be like a metaphor for cleaning up your life, for putting things back in their proper order. When you're done, you feel a real sense of accomplishment. Plus, as long as the house looks so nice, you might as well invite someone over.

Adopt a box turtle. Actually, getting any new pet will do, but I find exotic critters offer extra benefits. For instance, tracking them down can take days of research and phone calls, thereby occupying those idle hours with which you now find yourself. Then, too, there's the excitement of the pursuit and the satisfaction you feel when you finally locate the object of your desires. (Hmm. . . . Why does that sound so familiar?) But aside from filling up your time in a constructive fashion (Should I name her Sigourney? Or Shalala?), the obvious attraction is that you get a new focus for your affection, even if it's *not* exactly an equal trade.

Pretend you're John Cougar Mellencamp. Here's what you do: put on your favorite JCM CD (or any other rousing rock and roller), crank it way up, and sing along—maybe throwing in a little air guitar or dancing for good measure, as the mood strikes you. I don't know about you, but I find it nearly impossible to stay depressed while belting out a chorus or two of the "Authority Song," "Pink Houses," or "Serious Business." Not your most politically correct choice, perhaps, but maybe that's good: the less PC your musical selection, the more you are tapping into your rebelliousness.

Color your hair purple. If that seems too extreme to you (or your boss), try doing your hair the way "she" always hated it. This act functions as a declaration of independence, a reasonably mature way of sticking out your tongue. It is a way of making a statement to yourself and everyone else that you are your own self and not just half of a whole. Mostly, though, it's plain old fun.

Take a two-step class. This not only gives you something to do with your time, but it also gives you an opportunity to meet new people. The drawback to this is that you have to wear shirts with a lot of fringe and listen to country and western music. Actually, I am well on the way to recovery from the overdose of twang I suffered as a child, when every Saturday night my dad controlled the TV set and we watched "Hee Haw," "Nashville Tonight," "The Wilburn Brothers," and "The Porter Waggoner Show."

Order a lot of stuff from catalogs. This is a sure way to see that you get mail. Plus, by the time you receive the items you ordered, it's almost like getting a present. Of course, like the scooter/VCR gambit, it's a present you ultimately have to pay for.

What with all the practice I've had at this, I suspect I could easily come up with a number of other ways of boosting my self-esteem and generally pampering myself, but my plan is never to have to use survival techniques like these again. The way I figure it, Kath and I have been together now for about seven years, so we're pretty much home free. If you see any flaws in this plan, please don't tell me.

This Old Girlfriend

With middle age upon me, I've started thinking about growing old. Right off, you can tell I have started thinking about getting on in years because, for one thing, I am referring to myself as middle-aged. And I do so even though my dictionary says that mid-life is generally considered to be from forty-five to sixty-five or thereabouts. But the way I figure it is, if I only live to be eighty, then I'm already at the meridian of my life!

I suppose it sounds as though I'm obsessed by the age thing. But actually, it's more that I'm amused by everyone else's preoccupation with the traditional markers of advancing years—thirty, forty, fifty, and so on. Chronological measures of my length of time here on earth have never held any particular importance for me, probably because I'm so young at heart. Or soft in the head. Of course, technically, the two aren't mutually exclusive. . . . But to give an example of my relationship to age: I am nearly ten years older than my lover; and yet, we meet at about the same mental age of fourteen.

As a child, oddly enough, I was very old: at seven, getting my little sister off to school and cooking the occasional meal, by thirteen or fourteen, beginning to research which college to attend, and always, a nose-to-the-grindstone kind of student. And I stayed old, barring a few aberrant moments in high school and college, until my late twenties. Since then, however, I've been getting younger all the time. Let me tell you: my child within has *no* trouble finding its way out.

Still, there are definite signs that I am, in fact, getting older, indicators that cause me to chuckle at myself because some of them are the exact things I used to make fun of my parents and grandparents for doing or saying or believing. Karma is just so doggone funny.

To begin with, I have started to notice that the latest fashions only look sloppy to me. I know that, among the things lesbians have historically been known for, one of them is not being snappy dressers. Even so, the so-called styles of the last few years, both lesbian and straight, reflect a certain casualness that seems to me like a lapse from good grooming. During my own carefree youth, I was known to wear my share of t-shirts and frayed bell bottoms, but a shirt peeping out from under a sweater or jacket turns me into somebody's mother—it's all I can do to keep from yelling, "Tuck that shirt in, young lady." As for the grunge look, I'd be lying if I told you I've never commented, upon seeing some grunge band or other on *Saturday Night Live,* "I wonder if his mother is *proud* of him." Hairstyles, too, bring my encroaching crotchetiness to the surface. Much to my dismay I have found myself thinking thoughts like, "That young man would look very nice if he'd just cut his hair." My own hair—which my girlfriend has described (lovingly, I'm sure) as looking like Tammy Wynette's during her "Stand by Your Man" phase—is a far cry from the shaved heads of some of the baby dykes I know. Of course, even if I were so audacious as to sport a scalp with perpetual five o'clock shadow, it just wouldn't have the same effect without a pierced nose or lip or eyebrow to set it off. No, gone are the days of adventures in hair styling for me. Could we have a moment of silence, please, for my now long-departed purple tail. . . .

Also disconcerting is that I currently go through roughly a pound of moisturizer a month. I used to have skin that could've put the oil-producing nations out of business. In the last few years, I have found that if I don't slap generous amounts of lotion on every inch of my body after showering, I spend the rest of the day looking like a flea-infested dog. I use so much lotion that my lover is demanding her share of the cost be prorated.

Actually, taking a shower has become an altogether major production. It's not like the old days, when I could hop in, soap up, rinse off, towel dry, and dress. No sirree-bob. Now, I use one soap with an astringent just for my ears, which apparently are picking up the slack in oil production for the rest of my body. Then, I use another soap—this one with wheat germ oil—for the rest of my body. But not the face. Oh no, *not* the face. For my face, I now have to use a cucumber cleansing milk, otherwise my cheeks end up like fine-grade sandpaper. Then there's the coconut oil shampoo and the brazil nut hair conditioner, a generous dollop of gel to maintain my Tammy Wynette do, a slathering of lotion glopped all over my body, and the carrot moisture cream for my desert-like face. Aside from causing me to sound like the salad plate at a chichi restaurant, this regimen involves way more "beauty" products than I, as a crunchy dyke, am accustomed to dealing with. Frankly, it scares me a little. What's next—eye shadow? Oil of Olay? Electrolysis?

Even as moist as I am after all those goos and goops and creams, chances are that by midday, I will still be pawing at my clothes like a sitcom hillbilly, trying to alleviate an itch. The way I figure it, the only other moisturizing technique I have available to me right now—until they invent lotion-secreting clothing—is to get a wet suit, fill it with lotion, and climb into it for the night.

Another clear sign that I am, indeed, a mature woman is that I've been at the same job for over ten years. When I was in college, I held part-time jobs for as long as three or four years. Upon leaving those hallowed halls of newly molded cinder block, I had just an eensy bit of trouble deciding what it was I wanted to do when I grew up. Within the span of a couple of years I worked as an engineering technician, a technical writer, a bookstore clerk, and an advertising copy writer. "A long time on the job" in those days was about a year. Now I've been at the same job since 1981. Words like "retirement" and "pension" have been creeping into my vocabulary; I have outlasted several supervisors; and I am beginning to admit that I have "a career."

Yet another indication I am no longer of tender years is that my domicile has started filling up with Furniture, with a capital "F." Through my coed days and for many years thereafter, my furniture consisted of a double mattress and box spring on the floor, a lamp, a dresser, a few milk crates, and a single mattress with a throw thing over it and some foam cushions for a couch. My "home entertainment system" consisted of a tape player and a radio (two separate items) and a portable black-and-white TV you had to smack a few times on the side to get the volume adjusted properly. Now, furniture and electronic equipment cram every corner of our three-bedroom *house*. Besides a couch and a dining room table and normal grown-up home furnishings like that, I now have not only a cedar chest and a microwave cart but a chifforobe as well—I had never even heard that word before inheriting that particular piece of furniture. Worst of all, one of the things in life that *really* excites us is that we actually possess our very own washer and dryer. I remember when "an electrical appliance" meant maybe a toaster oven or a blender—something I could just throw in the trunk of the car when it was time to move again.

Further evidence of my approaching decrepitude is that these days the phrase "a late night out" means getting home a little after midnight. In my younger days, I sometimes didn't even go *out* until midnight. Now, it takes a very special occasion to get us to stay up past ten or eleven. And when we do, we're groggy, out of sorts, and feeling slightly hungover the whole next day. It's hard to imagine how we'd be if we had actually consumed alcohol!

I believe the technical term for people like us is "old farts." This does not bode well for Kath, who has just barely entered her thirties. I used to worry when we first got together, given the age difference thing, that she would at some point regret not having gotten to sow all of her wild oats. But I have to tell you, I'm pretty sure those wild oats are beyond dormant—they're kaput. When we're invited to parties that start at 8 or 9 p.m., Kathy whines about having to leave the house. I am much more stoic about the whole thing, and grimly calculate just how many diet Cokes I will need to consume to keep me from dozing off in some corner and embarrassing both of us by letting drool run down my chin. Don't get me wrong: it's not that we don't enjoy spending time with our friends. We do. It would just be nicer if they could come visit *us*—when we're at home in our jammies in bed—and if they wouldn't be offended when we nodded off. Sometimes I suspect I've been bitten by either a tsetse fly or Dracula. Maybe I just need some Geritol.

Much to my dismay, I have even started to dress for the weather. It used to be that my primary objective when selecting clothes from the closet was to look sharp, snappy—in a word: cool. Or at any rate, as cool as a puritanical white girl could. Back then, though, my personal thermostat seemed chronically set on high; cold weather bothered me hardly a'tall and so to dress fashionably was not to sacrifice personal comfort. I was always warmer than my lovers, and there was a constant struggle over who controlled the car temperature and the number of blankets on the bed.

Now, my blood seems just plumb worn out, and I am the one who is whining all winter long about how cold it is in the house. Consequently, I don't care how the hell I look when I go outside on those days when the thermometer dips below freezing, just as long as I'm warm. I now own a heavy flannel baseball cap with ear flaps and a pair of kickass Sorel boots (hunting boots good to forty below, for those of you uninitiated in the intricacies of cold weather wear), *and I wear them,* causing me, in the cold snap of 1994, to look a lot like Elmer Fudd on estrogen. On occasion, when the wind chill warrants, I have even been known to add, to this fab ensemble, some bunchy long underwear and the hood of my coat—over my cap. All of this leaves me, upon removal of my outer garments, in serious jeopardy of having a bad case of hat hair and looking like someone stuffed my clothing full of mashed potatoes. How I really know I'm getting old is, I am willing to take that risk.

Devastating for me, too, is that over the past few years I have started getting "ma'amed" by bag boys and store clerks. I have come to the conclusion I liked it better when they called me sir (that was pre-Tammy Wynette hair, of course). Equally comical is when a salesman or our neighbor refers to us as "ladies." "Ladies" are either a bunch of women playing bridge together and drinking tea or members of the royal family. The most genteel card game *I* know is poker, and the closest I get to royalty is my brother-in-law from upstate New York, whose last name is King.

Even my conversations are showing age lines—lines that irritated the hell out of me when my parents or grandparents used them. I can hardly believe it myself, but I have, in fact, begun saying things like, "When I was a kid, my parents would never have put up with that." Or, "When I was a kid, we were in bed by nine." Or, "I remember when postage stamps were only eight cents." It is for this reason, if no other, that I have decided I cannot have children. Before you know it, I would be saying things like, "Don't play with your feet at the table" and "Don't pick your nose in church—it's impolite" and "When I was your age, children knew better than to pierce their nostrils." There is no part of any of those phrases I would be happy to hear myself saying.

An even more disturbing turn to my conversations is

that they now often contain frank discussions of medical matter—not suitable for your more sensitive listener. The thing of it is, there's so much more to discuss now! The summer of '91 alone provided me with hours of material with which to bore my friends. That was the summer when, because Saturn was in Virgo with Scorpio rising and Pluto was in the dog house or some such equally scientific reason, I somehow ended up having a confluence of medical appointments.

Normally, my various annual and semi-annual checkups are routine and dull. And I've gotta say, that's pretty much the way I like it—an exciting Pap smear is something I can live without. In fact, if I ever *do* find a Pap smear exciting, I'd say it's time to examine the quality of my life. But all of my appointments that summer yielded the need for "a little something extra"—a phrase you might want to hear in conjunction with desserts or bonuses, but not from people in the medical profession. As the weeks wore on and I made my way dutifully from one white-coated woman to the next, I began to feel like somebody's rehab project.

"We could do a TV show," I commented to my younger and much less rickety girlfriend. "We could call it 'This Old Girlfriend.'"

> *This week on "This Old Girlfriend," we'll be looking at this fine old example of a medium frame girlfriend.*
>
> *Just how old would you say this structure is, Norm?*
>
> *Well, Steve, judging from the moldings and the creaking joints, I'd have to say somewhere right around World War II. You don't see too many like this anymore. Did you know, Steve, that this old girlfriend once had cleats and flat abs?*

I started the summer of '91 with a trip to the dentist, a lovely, wacky woman who must, like all dentists, have a very secure sense of self—how would *you* feel if everyone looked forward to seeing you with undisguised dread? And among the reasons we hate to visit the dentist is that they say insensitive things like, "You need a new crown." Hearing this news, my girlfriend quipped, "Couldn't you just eat some Imperial margarine? It would be much less expensive."

But aside from the fact that I hail from the dairy state and don't *do* margarine, I tend to go with more traditional medical care. So, in spite of my better judgment and despite knowing essentially what was in store for me, I actually returned to the dentist. In truth, though, aside from the expense, the worst part of the procedure was removing the old crown. To do this, she used something she called, whether officially or unofficially I'm not sure, "the clunker"—a big metal thing that looked more like a device for prying off fenders than something you would put in someone's mouth. Surprisingly enough, the whole thing was less than torturous. Still, I felt as though I should have had a bunch of those orange signs tacked on me to announce I was under construction.

Then came the annual gynie check-up, the humiliating experience we gals all love to hate. I don't know about you, but I find it hard to carry on a conversation about current events when someone is looking deeply into my vagina. And I never know whether to take my socks off or leave them on. Really, they don't get in the way of anything and it can often be on the chilly side in the examining room. On the other hand, don't you feel a bit silly wearing nothing but socks and a paper blanket draped over your lap? But who's to say what accessories are fashionable with a paper blanket?

Actually, all in all, I don't mind gynie visits that much. My internist is quite gentle and sensitive, and as long as we use the child-sized speculum I'm all right. The way things were going that summer, though, it shouldn't have surprised me that she would throw me a curve: "How about a cholesterol test? And while we're at it, why don't we test for anemia—your skin looks a little sallow." For the average grown-up, drawing a little blood is no big deal. But you have to bear in mind I am only masquerading as a grown-up. The truth is, I'm rather phobic about needles. I get queasy just seeing them on TV. Somehow, in spite of my natural fight-or-flight instinct, I managed neither to run from the lab technician nor to deck her.

But wait: there's more. This visit was followed by my biannual mammogram.

If you've never had a mammogram, here's what the experience is like. Imagine wearing nothing but a stylishly square-cut paper jacket on the top half of your torso. Then imagine some woman who is not your lover asking you to remove the jacket from your right side—Why do they do that? What is the point of covering up one breast when the other is completely exposed? Is having only one breast hanging out there somehow less humiliating than having both of them naked? In any case, once you've revealed the breast, be prepared: she will grab it, without so much as a how-do-you-do and place it carefully, like some sort of nouvelle cuisine, on a *cold* glass plate, rearranging it and your arm in a way that probably has nothing to do with artistic considerations. Then she lowers another cold hard surface down onto the top of your breast, squishing it flatter than you ever thought something that size could be squished—not, I suspect, that you've ever spent much time thinking about it prior to this experience. After she's assured herself that she's got an unbreakable choke hold on your breast, she says, "Don't breathe"—as if you could, clenching your teeth against the pain. Imagine having this procedure repeated three more times, for a total of two poses for each of your equally, I'm sure, photogenic breasts. The good thing, I guess, is that, for these pictures, you don't have to worry about whether your eyes were closed or your hair was a mess.

Finally, imagine, if you will, that the woman whose hands are roaming freely over your breasts is not a complete stranger—not someone, that is, whom you most likely will never see again. Neither is she your lover, who presumably touches your breasts frequently. Imagine, instead, she is someone whom you know slightly from the community, someone you are likely to encounter again casually at a reading or a dance. This is exactly what happened to me that ill-fated summer. What should merely have been a routine, somewhat uncomfortable medical procedure suddenly turned into an awkward social situation. Just what *do* you say to an acquaintance while she is squishing your breast?

I thought all of this was quite enough for one summer, thank you very much, but as usual, my decrepit body had other things in mind. To be specific, I had an unsightly mole on my back that needed to be removed. I didn't expect this to be a pleasant experience, of course, but I also was not expecting to be treated by Torquemada. Here's how it went: First, the doctor I had been sent to removed the band-aid protecting the ailing mole, whereupon she exclaimed rather forcefully, "Oh my *God!*" At which point, I am thinking, "Oh no: cancer for sure," until she added, "Boy, that's an ugly one." Then she explained the procedure to me: she would tie a string around the base of the mole which would cut off blood flow to it, thereby causing it to fall off of its own accord in a week or two. "I've had this procedure done myself," she shared, "and it hurts like hell." I inquired as to whether it wouldn't be possible to make use of one of the miracles of modern science—like anesthetic—to which she replied, "Wouldn't do a damn bit of good."

At this point, she had me lie face down on the examining table and clutch the edges, while she and a nurse stood on either side. This left no place for my girlfriend, who had come along for moral support, but the chair at my feet, watching my legs move up and down like a pain-o-meter. When the mole, much to everyone's surprise, came off in the nurse's hand, the doctor inquired, "Want to see it?" When I demurred, she said, "I wasn't talking to you—I was talking to your friend over there." At this point I was just happy to get away without the doctor's having suggested a blood letting or an application of leeches. I thought to myself, if I had known what this med school grad had had in mind—roping off my mole like a stubborn calf—we could've taken care of it at home with dental floss!

Thus ended that all too eventful summer, which *I* thought was destined to be the pinnacle of my medical adventures. But when I'm wrong, I'm really wrong. The summer of '93 easily topped my previous experience, with my girlfriend, my gynecologist, and me enacting not "This Old Girlfriend" but "Mystery Theater," trying to discover the source of the many mystifying symptoms I had apparently decided to exhibit. What my medical preoccupations lacked in variety in '93 compared with those of '91, they made up for in sheer intensity.

We began our search with an ultrasound. I was really grateful for this opportunity: having decided not to have children I thought this was an experience I would never get to have. And who *wouldn't* want the experience of drinking about a gallon of water and then not peeing for an hour or two while some guy presses down on your abdomen?

Next, my doctor wanted to do a laproscopy. For those of you unfamiliar with this procedure, pretend your doctor is a submarine captain and your innards are the deep blue sea. When the cap'n says, "Up periscope," it's your navel that the scope pokes into, allowing the commanding officer to have a look-see around for enemy vessels—in my case, endometriosis, which is *the* latest in women's diseases. This is not, by the way, what I had in mind whenever I've expressed a desire to be on the cutting edge. And for those of you not up on current trends, endo—as it is affectionately known—is basically the result of hunks of your uterine tissue wandering off to other parts of your body, settling there, menstruating, leaving scar tissue, and, incidentally, hurting like hell. I like to think that what happened is, my womb got bored hanging around doing pretty much nothing and took off on an intercorporeal Jack Kerouac thing. This, of course, is *exactly* how my doctor described the whole thing as well.

What really put my summer of '93 experiences over the top, though, was that the laproscopy resulted in a hospital stay. I felt like Gilligan must have when he boarded that boat for the three-hour tour: what was billed as same-day surgery ended up as a five-day odyssey. Being in the hospital was for me the medical version of *Mr.*

Toad's Wild Ride, but with twice the terror and half the fun.

In the prep room prior to surgery, an anesthesiologist to whom I had confessed my aversion to needles tried to distract me from the fact that two men wearing masks were busily trying to insert one into a vein on the back of my left hand. It was nice of him to try, but really, I can't imagine what he could have talked about that would have been riveting enough for me not to notice two people flopping my hand around like a fish and then spearing it.

My next memory was the face of my doctor, hovering over me like a vision. If I hadn't been in intense pain, this would have been a lovely experience as my doc is one cute number—brown eyes to die for and a great smile. My girlfriend, in fact, kiddingly says she had to get me out of the hospital because I was falling in love with my doctor, and my friends have been hinting broadly about transference. But the truth is, my doctor—and, after all, this is kind of important in someone you willingly allow to stand poised with a knife over your vital organs—is more than a pretty face. My adoration of her goes beyond that as well. To give but one example of her superiority as a medical professional and perhaps as a human being, she completely and totally accepted my girlfriend's involvement at every step of the presurgery and recovery processes. Though Kathy came to the hospital armed with her power of attorney, no one ever once asked for it. Cool. And that, my friends, in one paragraph, pretty much covers the high points of the hospital experience.

If a hospital wanted to adhere to a truth in advertising sort of code, it would post a sign at its doorway reading, "Abandon all hope of privacy and dignity all ye who enter here." But I suppose that would cut down on the visitor population some. The first of the indignities I had to suffer was being catheterized, with my little bag of pee hanging right out there for everyone to see. It's a disconcerting experience, to say the least, to have your friends know you are peeing when *you* don't even know you are! It did bring us closer together though.

Next came an alarming procession of doctors, most of whom I remember rather indistinctly, being in a morphine-induced haze. One guy, who reminded me of Colonel Klink with his bald head and German accent, seemed pretty hot on doing another surgery on me, so I kind of remember him. I also remember some doctor saying she needed to do an on-the-spot rectal exam. "You're kidding," I said. She wasn't. I have a sideways recollection of her as well. Most of the doctors just came in and asked to see my scar. At least I hope they were doctors. Because, after awhile, I got so blasé about the whole thing that I would pretty much lift my gown for anyone who asked.

Then there were the nightly visits from nurse C., whom I affectionately came to call "Nurse Ratchet"—although not to her face. I guess maybe we just got off to a bad start. At midnight the first night, she came into my room to rearrange my bed table (tidiness knows no time, I guess) and to tell me I must sit up and cough up my "sputum." I replied indignantly that I didn't *have* any sputum. "You may think you don't, but you do," she retorted rather testily, then slammed a few more things around and left the room. I listened for a key in the door lock, but I guess she figured if I didn't have the oomph to sit up and take care of my sputum I wasn't in any danger of running away or starting a mutiny.

As it turned out, Nurse Ratchet was in the minority.

Most of my nurses were quite wonderful. I think they kind of liked me. I didn't cuss them out the way my crabby roommate did, and I made them laugh. Like the time two of them entered the room wearing rubber gloves. "Oh-oh," I said. "*Two* people wearing rubber gloves: this can't be a good sign." I also exchanged pleasantries with them as I did laps of the ward, my hand encircling my I.V. pole like the hand of a secret friend.

Probably the worst indignity of all was having to suffer through six—count 'em: *six*—enemas before going for a colonoscopy. Fortunately for all concerned, at least I didn't have a roommate at that point in time. I said to a friend of mine later, "I can't believe some people actually do enemas for pleasure."

"Yeah, and pay for them," she commented. Then, after a pause, she added, "Oh. I guess you'll be paying for it too. . . ."

After the whole enema thing, the colonoscopy was almost anticlimactic, except that it is a *little* weird to be lying there with a group of people gathered around your bare butt watching the inside of your colon on a TV screen as though it were an especially riveting episode of *Upstairs, Downstairs*. "What a way to make a living," I commented to the technician at the end of the show. She laughed and said, "Yep, that's all we do here—butts and guts."

As it turned out, based on the second opinion we asked for, we decided I didn't need to undergo the second surgery. Or at least not right away. But given that the surgeon who proffered the second opinion was this way cool dyke doctor, my girlfriend decided on the spot that if I ever did need a second surgery, we would assemble an all-lesbian surgical team, and we didn't figure we'd have much trouble doing it. "Now all we need is a lesbian anesthesiologist," Kathy commented.

To which a friend of ours replied, "Or, maybe by the time you're ready for the other surgery, one of the male anesthesiologists will have undergone a sex change operation and become a lesbian. Then you'll have to decide if you want a woman-born woman only team." I'm hoping we won't be engaged in that debate any time soon.

Actually, although my belly looks a little like either a football or a trussed turkey (we can't decide which), I'm recovering quite nicely and, having left the hospital, have reclaimed most of my dignity. I am now also a proud member of the Endometriosis Association, although, much to my girlfriend's chagrin, we did not receive with our first mailing, as she had hoped, a t-shirt reading, "My girlfriend got endometriosis and all I got was this lousy t-shirt." She did brighten when we learned my doctor had recommended, of all things, birth control pills for keeping the endo in check. "Our love-making," she quipped to friends, "is so much freer now that we don't have to worry about unwanted pregnancy." One of these friends cautioned Kathy actually to be careful lest I was only *pretending* to take my pills and was trying to trap her into having to marry me. Fortunately, Kathy trusts me.

Since then, though, in the aftermath of all the surgical hoopla, things have been a tad dull around here. But to be honest, we kind of like it that way. It gives me time to moisturize.

What The Nielsens Don't Know (And We'd Rather Not Admit)

One of the earliest known photographs of moi, chronicler of lesbian life ordinaire, shows me standing in the empty husk of one of those big old 1950s prototype TVs, my eighteen-month-old face displaying, over a series of several photographs, the range of personalities one might find on the tube normally occupying that space. It is to this experience that I trace my profound lifelong connection to the television medium. I don't know what excuse all you other dykes out there are using, but that's mine. You'll have to get your own.

Because clearly, I am not the only lesbian in town who has bonded with this animatedly inanimate object. Lesbians, of course, are prone to the same pitfalls of popular culture as the rest of the U.S. population—if you sell us mouthwash, do we not gargle?—but you'd think that with the scant few images to be had of us on TV we'd be a little more resistant to its spell. *Au contraire, mon frères and frèrettes:* we lesbians have been just as entranced with TV as every other red-blooded American of our TV-era generations.

Sometimes being a member of this larger culture overwhelms not only our lesbian feminism but our common sense as well, and TV-viewing habits are certainly one example of this. There are probably more dykes among us who could join in on a rousing rendition of the theme songs from "The Addams Family," "The Flintstones," and "Gilligan's Island" than any song you could name by women's music stars such as Cris Williamson or Holly Near. Of course, the former tunes were consumed, along with Wonder Bread, during our formative years, and most of us have had a change in consciousness—not to mention bread products—since then.

Or so most of us would argue. However, at least within my broad circle of friends and acquaintances, I have seen evidence to the contrary—evidence, that is, not that our consciousness hasn't changed since the days when we were all singing "Hey, hey, we're the Monkees," but that consciousness goes down the tube when it comes to TV.

This hasn't always been true. When I was first coming out—back when PC had only one meaning and it wasn't "personal computer"—TV viewing was valued in much the same way as were shaven legs, roast beasts, and male puppies: it was frowned upon. Sure, to this day there are still those among us who scorn TV (I actually have one or two friends who don't even *own* a TV), but the days of denying the effect of our Wonder Bread Years have thankfully passed. Still, do we have to continue to watch *bad* TV? With all the witty, socially conscious programs available to us today, do we have to continue to watch squishy, white, nutritively bankrupt TV? Apparently, the answer is yes.

I am here to tell you that large numbers of lesbians have confessed to watching reunion episodes of shows such as "Eight Is Enough," "Dobie Gillis," and "The Brady Bunch"—and don't try to pretend you're not one of them. At that party where the hostess turned off the music to watch "The Brady Bunch" reunion, I don't recall having to teach *you* the theme song before we joyfully belted it out with everyone else. . . .

Obviously, reunion shows are not really "new" shows, and one may be tempted to interpret the above instances as a spate of ugly nostalgia for our fading youth. Seventies trash becomes eighties camp. Maybe it's only that we were all simply curious about how our TV peers—kids we sometimes knew better than our own siblings—had turned out. Unfortunately, the truth of the matter is that we are not *only* looking back fondly at our primordial TV pasts.

Now I hate to make this one of those kiss-and-tell books, but my lover, my hairdresser Frank, and more than one of our friends have all been, at one time or another in the very recent past, hooked on "All My Children," each of them having been aided and abetted by TV's sidekick, the VCR. The temptation is to chalk this up to the idiosyncrasies of a few individuals. But as I found out, this particular viewing flaw is shared by many lesbians. At a barbecue once, women we didn't even know—lured, evidently, either by my silent charm or by the fervent tones of my darling Kathy and two of our friends—flocked around to join in on a passionate discussion of "All My Children."

Why "All My Children" above all others? Why were lesbians not equally passionate about "One Dysfunctional Life to Live" or "The Young and the Useless" or "Another Totally Heterosexist World" or any of all those other soaps there are to choose from? According to Kathy, who started watching "AMC" in college because her four housemates were fans, "All My Children" has been popular with a lot of lesbians because about ten years ago, the show had a lesbian on it. Apparently, they are still hoping she will come back.

This can't have been the case for our friend Susan, who has been a fan since grade school, when, in the days before VCRs, she had her mother tape the show for her on her *cassette recorder* so she could listen to it when she got home. Somehow, I picture her walking home from school with a lunch box sporting the faces of Palmer, Erica, and the gang with bold letters spelling out "All My Children." Surely, no such lunch box could have existed, right? Given that my girlfriend, when in first grade, had a "Laugh In" lunch box, I can't really be certain about this.

All of this is not to say that I am above watching junk TV myself, that—in spite of what you might believe about my viewing habits given my intimate knowledge of Endora's family tree—I am an ardent fan of PBS and PBS only. In reality, I have been known to watch "Mr. Belvedere," "Growing Pains," and "Puttin' on the Hits." In my own defense, I'd like to say I am seldom actually *watching* such shows—the TV just happens to be tuned to those stations while I'm cooking or cleaning. I draw the line, however, at "Three's Company" and "All-Star Wrestling"—which accounts for the light dusting of flour on the portable TV screen and the hint of egg glaze on the channel knob.

It would be all well and good if this dreck were the sum of one's TV-viewing options because then one might reasonably hope to make TV a smaller part of one's life. But there is actually so much *good* TV these days that it's hard to find the time to truly talk to one's partner; commercials just aren't long enough to give any kind of thorough consideration to whether you should open your relationship up and become nonmonogamous or who will actually bear your first child. Even so—even taking into account the high quality of shows such as "Murphy Brown," "Picket Fences," "Roseanne," "Mad about You," "I'll Fly Away," and so on—what is it about TV that *lesbians* find so appealing? Aside from, that is, the likes of Katie Couric.

In the old days, of course, there simply were no lesbians on TV. Therefore, we had to make them up: Betty and Wilma, Lucy and Ethel, Miss Hathaway, Alice from "The Brady Bunch." Obviously, judging from the above cast of characters, we were a desperate people. Today, assuredly, in these much more enlightened and tolerant times, things are drastically different on the old Trinitron: there is one semiregular lesbian character on one TV show who may actually, in real life, be an actual lesbian, depending on which late-night TV talk show you tune into and when. I am, of course, referring to Peppermint Patty. No, I really meant Nancy, Sandra Bernhard's character on "Roseanne," but isn't Peppermint Patty just the cutest little butch thing you'd ever want to meet?

The truth is, until Nancy came along with her gorgeous girlfriends—first Morgan Fairchild and then Mariel Hemingway (and who says TV's not realistic!)—the lesbians appearing on sitcoms and dramas were nearly all one-night stands: on the show one night, maybe two, then never seen or heard from again. Don't get me wrong—some of these were great one-night stands and whenever a rumor started circulating about a dyke surfacing on a show, a phone network would instantly spring up, making sure no one missed out on the momentous occasion.

These appearances being few and far between, though, most often we watched shows in which *we* recognized a certain character as being a lesbian; we were merely waiting for the show's writers to realize it. Remember Buddy on "Family"? I *still* think the show was just canceled before she had a chance to come out. . . . As it turns out, if one is to believe the tabloids at any rate, the actress who played her is now a lesbian—a lesbian who, according to one report by a supposed ex-lover, liked to bark while having sex. This has caused me, during my most cynical and morally corrupt days as a writer, to contemplate doing a biography: "Bark Like a Dog: The Kristy McNichol Story."

The thing of it is, we never give up hope that certain characters will one day come out, even on shows already in syndication. The truth is, what we'd all secretly like to see is an issue of *TV Guide* like this one:

Sunday

"Murder, She Wrote." Mrs. J. B. Fletcher (Angela Lansbury) reveals the mystery of how she manages to write, travel, solve puzzling cases, and still find time to bake and keep an immaculate house: Miss R. Hall (Mary Tyler Moore), her live-in secretary and long-time companion.

Monday

"Love and War." When Meg (Suzie Plakson) is sent by the newspaper to cover the Gay Games, a whole new world opens up to her. Dana (Annie Potts) cooks her a special meal of scrambled tofu, lentil cutlets, and a Sharps.

"Northern Exposure." Ruth-Anne dumps recent beau Walt when she is swept off her feet by one of Marilyn's aunts. When the whole town starts talking about it, Ed (Darren E. Burrows) decides to shoot a documentary called "Go Dish." Marilyn: Elaine Miles.

Tuesday

"Oprah." Topic: Lesbians who lead perfectly boring and "normal" lives.

"Roseanne." Nancy (Sandra Bernhard) visits Darlene in Chicago and takes her to a gay bar, Orlando's. Darlene suddenly realizes why she had been putting off having sex with David for so long. Darlene: Sara Gilbert.

Wednesday

"Home Improvement." Tim's guests on "Tool Time," in a recurring role, are the women who build the stages and put up the tents at the Michigan Womyn's Music Festival. Al and Jill (Patricia Richardson) comment on Tim's more numerous than usual macho grunts. Tim: Tim Allen.

Thursday

"Late Night with Kate Clinton." Kate's guests include Jodie Foster, Whitney Houston, and Rush Limbaugh (Stupid Hetero Tricks). Featuring Melissa Etheridge and the World's Most Dangerously Dykey Band.

Friday

"Picket Fences." When Kimberly decides one kiss with another woman was not really much of a test and runs off to Doe Farm, Jimmy (Tom Skerritt) goes off half-cocked, accuses the separatists at the farm of brain-washing her, and takes them to court. Douglas Wambaugh defends the "butch little man-haters."

Saturday

"Family Ties." Jennifer (Tina Yothers) discovers that not only does she like basketball but she has an affinity for softball and rugby as well. "Team spirit" takes on a whole new meaning for her.

In the meantime—until this issue of *TV Guide* or some variation of it appears, and because women's basketball games are seldom televised and roller derby has long since left the airwaves—we'll all just have to get our fix of lesbians on TV by watching "Roseanne," "American Gladiators," and "Rescue 911." However, even when we do start seeing regular gay and lesbian characters on sitcoms, that happenstance will not mark the pinnacle of our acceptance by straight America. No—not until Madison Avenue starts courting us with TV commercials will we know that we've reached that high point.

Think about it: Civil Rights Laws were passed in the sixties; in the seventies, we *finally* started seeing African-American politicians getting elected and we saw *some* African-American sitcoms and a few more diverse roles for African-Americans in movies—if you count "Good Times" and *Shaft* as progress, that is. But not until the mid-eighties or so did we begin to see African-American folks in toothpaste, car, and deodorant commercials—as if all people of African descent had been opting not to brush their teeth and were taking public transportation until then. The truth of the matter is that companies and their ad agencies, though they'd probably never admit it, were worried that, at best, white America would not be able to identify with African-American product users (and therefore not buy the product) and, at worst, racist white America would form negative associations between African-Americans and the product (and therefore not buy it). Then, too, some of what was behind the noticeable absence of dark-skinned people in commercials was racism of the most insidious kind: they just never thought of putting nonwhites in their commercials.

Well in a way, that's what's still happening with the advertising world and gays and lesbians. The situation is not completely analogous, of course (for a variety of reasons), but to paraphrase an old saying, "Some of my best friends are gays and lesbians—but I wouldn't want them selling my product." Oh sure, there's one furniture place that shows a gay male couple buying their products and a K-Mart commercial K-Mart denies was meant to be gay oriented. And there has also been an impressive array of print ads for big name products—mostly designed to run in gay and lesbian publications. For the most part, though, it would appear advertisers feel middle America is not quite ready yet for the likes of us to come into their homes and talk to them about feminine itching, coffee stains on one's boxer shorts, furniture polish, and athlete's foot. And they may be right. Yet, I feel confident that, in the not too distant future, we'll be seeing commercials like the following:

The scene: A rapid montage of women sitting in front of performers on a stage, lounging together before a backdrop of tents, shopping at outdoor stalls, eating plates of tofu and veggies, etc.

Voiceover: Every year five thousand women come to the Michigan Womyn's Music Festival for five days of music, workshops, relaxing, shopping, and eating bland food. But if you're going to go to the festival, you better leave your husbands and sons at home and you better bring your Visa card, because they don't allow men and they don't take American Express. Visa. It's every place you want to be.

Well, maybe that's a little too exotic for the average American TV viewer. Perhaps it would be better to start with something a little more familiar—like the neighborhood bar.

The scene: A bar with a number of women in softball garb milling around and men sitting on bar stools in couples. A TV is playing at the end of the bar. A good-natured argument erupts.

Woman #1: Let's watch the softball tournament at the Gay Games on ESPN. [Reaches over and switches channel to softball game.]

Man #1: No—the drag show on the gay channel. [Switches to a beautifully coiffured and begowned man lip synching to "I'm Every Woman."]

Woman #2: Softball. [Switches back.]

Man #2: Drag show. [Changes channel again.]

All women: Softball! [Someone turns it to the game again.]

All men: Drag show! [Back to lip synching.]

The bartender: Let's watch both. [Bonks the TV set with a bottle of Miller Lite. Suddenly, the screen fills with women in frilly dresses, makeup, and splendid jewelry playing softball.]

Voiceover: Miller Lite. If you can combine great taste with less filling, you can combine anything.

But now that I think about it more, I'm not sure they'd use this one—isn't the point of these commercials that the end result is something you would never see? Well, something like that last TV scene actually took place in the summer of 1994 when a team of lipstick lesbians, the Tarts, took the field in the Metropolitan Softball Association's women's recreational league. In fact, I heard that during one game the other team even allowed a guy wearing a skirt to join the Tarts so they wouldn't have to forfeit—what better proof do you need that you can, indeed, combine drag and softball? On the other hand, I'm going to guess it's not *all* that common of a scene. . . .

Maybe a better way to begin our foray into the world of TV advertising is with more homey products—dishwashing liquid, microwave cake mixes, and power tools. How about this, for instance?

The scene: An old-fashioned kitchen, filmed with sepia overtones. A woman with bobbed hair wearing a 1940s style dress and apron stands at a washtub, rubbing a Rockford Peaches baseball uniform on a washboard.

Voiceover: [woman's voice] For centuries, we've been rubbing stains out of clothes.

[The scene shifts to a modern-day laundry room.]

Voiceover: [woman's voice] Now it's easier. Introducing Spray 'n Wash Gel.

[A woman holds up a badly stained rugby shirt. Another woman, wearing basketball shoes and uniform, passes through the back of the room, bouncing a basketball. She waves. The first woman smiles and shakes her head in a bemused fashion. Close up of first woman scrubbing stain on rugby shirt.]

Voiceover: [woman's voice] Finally, a stain remover with enzymes and a fabric-safe brush that removes those stains—like blood and grass—that ruin clothes.

[Close up of the product.]

Voiceover: [man's voice] Spray 'n Wash Gel gets out what America gets into.

If that commercial isn't cozy enough for you, try this one:

The scene: A nicely decorated nursery lit warmly by sunlight streaming in through a window. Two women lean over a crib, then stand facing the camera, their arms lightly around one another's waists. An infant of a different race stirs sleepily in the crib.

First woman: We want what's best for our baby.

Second woman: We don't want to give our baby just any formula. Carnation has all of the nutrients our baby needs. And pediatricians recommend it, so you know it's good.

[The women lean over the crib again and stroke the baby's back and head. They look up at each other and smile tenderly. Then a shot of the product comes on the screen with the first woman saying, "Remember: mother's milk is best." Second woman: "But when neither of you can breastfeed, Carnation is the next best thing to mother's milk." Both women: "Carnation formula: because we want what's best for our baby."]

Personally, I don't see how you could get much sweeter or more homey than that. Maybe it's a little *too* sweet for some—like the right-wing kooks who don't think lesbians should *have* children. But surely they can't object to us having telephones, can they?

The scene: A woman decked out in Gap Wear, Doc Martens, and freedom rings stands in front of an urban house.

Voiceover: You are a lesbian. You have a lover who runs a women's coffeehouse, with performers to schedule, boxes of herbal tea to order, cotton t-shirts to be printed with the coffeehouse logo.

[The scene shifts to an interior. The freedom-ring-wearing woman listens to answering machine message: "Hello, this is Spike? From Your Butch Older Sister? The band, you know? Um, we were wondering if an 8:30 starting time is, like, cast in stone? Because we don't really hit our stride until about 11:30, you know?" (Woman listening rolls her eyes.)]

Voiceover: You need VoiceMail from Ameritech.

I am cooking here with these commercials, don't you think? In fact, I may call my lawyer and see what my chances are of collecting royalties when these ads hit the airwaves. Okay, maybe it's not very likely—but it's possible.

And that, I think, is the real appeal of TV to lesbians: it is a world where anything is possible, a world where murders can be solved in an hour (not counting commercials), where a saccharine purple dinosaur can have the appeal of the Beatles to the under five set, where someone is made completely unrecognizable to his co-workers by exchanging tights and a cape for a suit and glasses, where Suzanne Somers can be a star. In a world like this, lesbians could be next-door neighbors to the Huxtables, mothers raising children, daughters who are still integral members of their biological families, regular characters leading regular sitcom lives. TV is just weird enough for something like that to happen. I sure hope it happens soon, too, because it's getting harder and harder to believe Buddy on "Family" will be coming out any day now—especially since the show has been canceled for over a decade.

Adventures In TherapyLand

I am no stranger to therapy. Believe it or not, I was once horribly neurotic. But after a year or two of therapy, off and on—why, now I'm delightfully neurotic. Or so I like to think. A dissenting opinion on the "delightful" part can be heard, I'm sure, from my girlfriend, family, and friends. But as I used to say to my mom, if I wasn't a little crazy, I'd go insane. It seems to me that normality, like any other good thing, can be carried too far. Look at Ward and June Cleaver—they were supposedly as normal as anything. And they were as bland as mashed potatoes with no gravy.

The Cleavers may have been on the bland side, but Wally and Beaver—or so the presumption goes—grew up to be healthy, happy, well-adjusted adults. Although, really, how well-adjusted *can* someone be whose life-long appellation refers to a large-toothed soggy rodent? Most of us did not grow up in such a blissfully bland household. My own family, for instance, was less like the Cleavers and more like *The Beverly Hillbillies* meets *Knots Landing*, with a little of *The Addams Family* thrown in for color—and without all that messy money to muddy things up. Yes, it's true: I, too, am the product of the ever-popular dysfunctional family. Time-tested, father-approved. Incest, the emotionally absent father, physical abuse—these are just some of the things offered to the lucky graduate of the nuclear family, that commodity so highly prized by the "Moral" Majority (don't make me hurl!). Is it any wonder some of us need a little help unscrambling our brains? And then, add to the "normal" stuff of growing up in a dysfunctional family the confusion of being gay or lesbian in a homophobic society—well, doctor, when does my fifty minutes begin?

Finding a good and/or compatible therapist, however, is not always so easy. And a bad therapist (or a bad match) can be worse than no therapist at all. Fortunately, way back when I was a therapy virgin, I got very lucky—without breaking any therapist/client boundaries, that is. Actually, I may have been too lucky—by which I mean that I don't know if, like a baby dyke—oops: Freudian slip—if like a baby *duck* I was at the imprinting stage or what, but I've never been able to waddle off and find another therapist with whom I work as well as the first one.

Having emerged from a household in which the father figure (i.e., the figure of my stepfather) didn't believe in therapy—as if we were talking about the Tooth Fairy or S. Claus—but believed, instead, that one should pull oneself up by one's own bootstraps (a gravity-defying feat in actual practice), it is doubtful I would ever have sought therapy out. As it happened, I ended up in therapy kind of by accident. Here's how it came to pass: One day in Milwaukee, I went to the student health center at my university, complaining of a sore throat. While there, I noticed the name of a new psychologist posted among the undistinguished names of all the other staff. The name was that of my former psych statistics T.A., on whom, it just so happens, I had had a wicked crush. I stopped in to see her under the pretext of congratulating her on having completed her Ph.D. By way of conversation, she asked me how I was doing. I, by way of an answer, burst into tears. And the rest, as they say, is therapeutic history.

Actually, I got at least two things from being in therapy with Dr. K that bear mentioning. The first was learning to put things in perspective. To illustrate, I offer the following statement from Dr. K: "Now let me get this right—You have no friends, no pets, no TV or stereo, you're broke, you live in a tiny studio apartment downwind from the tannery and have to put buckets out all over the room when it rains—and you wonder why you're *depressed?*" Oh. Now I get it.

The other thing I got from Dr. K was the wonderful diagnostic assessment: "You wouldn't be happy if they hung you with a new rope," which has provided me with years of entertainment, trying to figure out what the hell that *means.* But whatever it means, I'm sure she was right: Dr. K was perfect. A little transference going on? What? Who me? Naw. Just because I never got over the fact that she didn't follow me when I left Milwaukee doesn't mean I was experiencing any *transference.*

But the truth is, I never did find such a good therapist/client match again. Then again, maybe I did and just didn't know it. Comedian Margaret Smith does a joke about therapy in which she ponders how you know whether you really have a good therapist. "Does your therapist have a balloon business on the side?" she asks the crowd anxiously. Well, none of my therapists had a helium tank sitting in the corner or anything, but that doesn't mean I didn't sometimes feel like I was at some sort of carnival—the carnival of souls, I think.

Dr. S practiced out of her home, an unassuming, typical sort of structure on a typical sort of tree-lined street. At least she said it was her house. I never actually saw more than the sun porch where her office was, although I did sometimes hear male voices, presumably those of her husband and son, coming from the other end of the hallway. And I have to admit that her office wasn't terribly office-like, with plants and artwork everywhere and a series of couches and chairs arranged into a "conversation pit." Still, that's the sort of thing therapists do: create a homey atmosphere to put you at ease—as if you could be comfortable in any type of setting while describing to a perfect stranger how sleeping with an old softball mitt left behind by your ex-girlfriend is somehow comforting. There was one session, though, that did offer up pretty strong evidence that there were, in fact, living quarters in the part of the place I never saw.

It was the time I arrived for my session desperately needing to use the facilities, just a few steps beyond the glass-paned door of her office. No problem: I simply had to share the space with her five-year-old daughter, who would be taking a bath on the other side of the drawn shower curtain—drawn for whose privacy, I'm not sure. Do you know how hard it is to pee with a total stranger sitting quietly and nakedly not more than four feet away from you? As if that wasn't bad enough, I then discovered there was no more toilet paper on the roll. While contemplating what social etiquette might dictate to do about this dilemma, Dr. S slipped her hand into the room with a new roll. I was less than at ease for our session.

Another time, as I worried over what effect my breast biopsy scar might have on my dating life, Dr. S graciously offered to assess my scar and to let me take a look at her own. Before I could say "Pop goes the suture," her breast was right there, in front of my disbelieving eyes. I was so taken aback, I have no recollection of what sort of blouse she had on or her undoing any kind of bra—it all happened so fast. Like an accident. Her bare breasts, however, are forever burned into my memory. I know she meant well, but a provincial gal like myself just isn't used to authority figures disrobing in her presence. Not since Clifford and I were behind the garages at the projects, when I was about eight, had I played "I'll show you mine if you'll show me yours." I shudder to think what might have transpired if my concern had been with an episiotomy.

One of my most recent therapy experiences involved no literal baring of breasts, but I had a funny feeling of exposure nonetheless. The sessions in question were with Dr. j, which I'll spell with a small "j" so you don't confuse her with the basketball player, like I know you would otherwise. Anyway, Dr. j's sparsely furnished office—three leather director-type chairs, a small crate of children's toys, and two small end tables, one bearing a telephone (next to what was clearly the doctor's chair) and the other bearing a box of tissues (between what were clearly the client's chairs)—was also equipped with one of those two-way mirrors. On the other side of the mirror was another therapist who would occasionally sit and phone in questions for Dr. j to ask the client—i.e., me. I felt like I was in one of those old movies about Greek mythology—you know, where the Gods sat up in the clouds and moved the mere mortals below as though they were chess pieces? And even though I knew the "cloud" in this case was only a piece of glass and that probably no one back there was named Zeus, I kept expecting to be turned into a swan or to have babies come bursting out of my forehead or something.

The other "tool" Dr. j used was a video camera, with which she recorded all of our sessions. This, she said, was to help her remember all that transpired. "Oh sure," my girlfriend responded skeptically when I told her of this arrangement. And then she moaned, "You're going to end up on 'Hard Copy'!" More likely "America's Funniest Neurotics," I suspected. Between the mirror, the video camera, and Dr. j's eagerly receptive face, I had a hard time, as you might imagine, deciding exactly where I should be looking. Naturally, I generally looked directly at the radiator on the right side of the room.

I have also had a therapist whom I went to see only once—a sort of therapeutic one-night stand, I guess. There was just no chemistry, you know? Like a duet between Melissa Etheridge and Wayne Newton maybe. Given that we'd only been together for fifty minutes, I didn't think I had any moral obligations beyond leaving a message that I wouldn't be keeping my next appointment—or any others, for that matter. That, I thought, was the end of it. But I made the valuable discovery that quitting your therapist is like breaking up with someone: leaving a message just won't do. She called me back, apparently feeling the need to process, to understand why it was I didn't want to see her anymore after just one "date." And the woman wasn't even a lesbian, for heaven's sake. The only good point about it was at least we didn't have any property to divvy up.

Adding up these different experiences, though, I'd have to say I did come away, in the end, with new insights. Like did you ever realize how when the client before you comes out, you look discreetly away, even though you're dying to know what this person looks like and what the hell *her* problem is that she needs a *therapist?* And did you ever notice whatever chair you sit in at your first session is the chair you use for the entire rest of the time you continue to see that therapist? Of course, couples counseling can throw a different dynamic into the whole chair thing. When my lover Kathy and I went, we decided after a session or two that one seat in particular seemed to be the "hot seat"—that is, whoever sat there was more closely and nerve-wrackingly scrutinized by the therapist. Thereafter, upon entering the room, we would race for the non–hot seat, elbowing each other aside—in that friendly, mature sort of way that characterizes our relationship. The therapist, I think, lost all hope at that point.

These insights aside, what I've just recounted here is the therapy version of serial monogamy: limited forays, one after another, into the wacky fun-filled world of psychological counseling. But in some parts of the lesbian community, the most stable relationships you'll find are those between a lesbian and her therapist. Therapists have taken on an almost higher-being quality in the lesbian community. So great is our belief in therapy that we lesbians not only go individually but also, as I have alluded, as couples—and, in many cases, as ex-couples—and sometimes even *before* we're a couple. I feel it is only fair to confess I have participated, however briefly, in all three types of these couples counselings.

Couples counseling, you may be thinking, is not so weird—married people frequently seek out such counseling. Relationships are stressful, people grow and change, become disillusioned with one another—couples counseling, you think, makes some sense. But *ex-couples* counseling?

Well, it's a widely known fact that lesbians frequently stay friends with their ex-lovers. Unfortunately, sometimes they just can't figure out real well how to do that. Some of the same crap that bugged the hell out of you when you were together can still bug you when you're not—for instance, when she says, "I'll call you later," "later" might mean in two hours—or in two weeks. And then there are whole new arenas to explore—like, How could you leave me for *her?* And: When you give me a hug now, does that just mean you want to hug, or does it mean you want to, um, you know? So even though you've *both* (yeah, right) decided you just want to be friends, there's still a fair amount that needs to be sorted out. Why bother sorting, you say? If you're split up, you're split up—that's it. Well, that's not the way many lesbians figure it—and that's just one of the many things that make us so special.

There are two other considerations with this ex-lovers counseling thing. One is, if both of you are going to continue to hang out in the same circles—and chances are you will, the lesbian community being the inspiration for Disneyland's "Small World" exhibit—you need to learn how to be in the same room with each other without picking up a meat cleaver or keening sorrowfully at the moon. Such actions can be disturbing to those around you—not to mention to each other. The second consideration that enters in these days—something most people thought they'd never be hearing lesbians say—is, What about the children? That is, lesbians who have kids together and have decided to continue to coparent even though they no longer cohabit must, like many a divorced hetero couple, learn how to pretend to be grown-ups during the ritual passing back and forth of the children on weekends. This is where your friendly local therapist comes in.

So you might be willing to buy the ex-couples counseling, but what about counseling for couples who aren't even a couple yet? Well, all I can say is that, as ex–Girl Scouts, many of us lesbians try to be prepared for anything. In our case, Kathy and I had unwittingly fallen (one of us less unwittingly than the other, I'd have to say in all honesty) onto the bobsled course of monogamy and were trying to figure out a way off—or at least a way to slow down the momentum. Hell, who were we trying to kid? We were already buying groceries together and might as well have been keeping the other apartment as a summer home—if it hadn't been for the fact that it was roach-infested and disgusting. Nevertheless, we were trying to be responsible about getting involved and so decided to allay our fears about that involvement by seeing a therapist.

Unfortunately, we only made it to one session. The problem was, sitting there in front of the therapist, Kathy suddenly got couch fright. Or at any rate, she seemed to have lost the power of speech. I felt like a ventriloquist, telling the therapist what Kathy felt, what Kathy wanted, and what Kathy would say if she were capable of speech, while Kathy nodded her head dumbly in confirmation, a look in her eyes like Baby Jessica in the well. To this day, I'm sure that therapist worries Kathy had fallen under the spell of a domineering older woman. Well, she'd be half right, anyway; I do sort of have an enchanting personality. . . . In the end, we jettisoned therapy altogether and stumbled blindly into a relationship like every other red-blooded American lesbian.

Of course, the stumbling part was pretty much our own fault—there must have been a self-help book out there somewhere that addressed our dilemma. There are self-help books for everything, aren't there? *Healing the Three Stooges Fan Within; Now That You Know—A Guide to Running Screaming from the Room; The Big Hair Syndrome; No More Barbie Bashing: Confronting the Feminist Censor Within; A Nintendo Duck-Hunting Plan for Your Inner Child; Opening the Door to a New Fuller Brush Man; Healing with Chicklets; Learning to Say Whoa: Putting the Brakes on Your Monogamous Bobsled Slide*—if we had only taken a trip to our local feminist bookstore, I'm sure we would have found something there to enlighten us. Self-help books may be generally hot right now, but lesbians are among the biggest buyers, I'm sure. If we don't help ourselves, who will? And we've been doing it for years. . . .

I am sure our avid readership of self-help books is at least partially responsible for the illustrious career of co-dependency, and other faddish problems: we were healing spiritually—New Age religion, crystals, the whole ball of feathers—before most heteros too. And then there's The Child Within—almost nobody even knew theirs was missing until lesbians started looking all over the place for their own. Although, I don't quite get this one: most lesbians *I* know pretty much have their child right there on the outside where everybody can see it. Who else do you think is buying all those softballs, train sets, Pee Wee Herman dolls, electric hockey games, and Brady Bunch memorabilia you see cluttering the shelves and tables of lesbian households?

Like self-help books, another area of the lesbian self-improvement mania I haven't explored are 12-step programs. Consequently, I know very little about them—except what I pick up through the buzz around the community. So here's my impression of the 12-step groups frequented by lesbians, based on those little snippets:

1. 12-step programs are like the Rosicrucians, the Masons, the Nihilists (of turn-of-the-century Russia), or some other exotic secret organization: no one outside the group is supposed to know who else is in the group and, for safety's sake, only first names are used.

2. 12-step programs in the community are like big dating services. This makes no sense to me in light of another thing I've heard about the program—that participants are encouraged not to date at all during their first year in AA (so they can concentrate on getting/staying sober). But couples are always turning up who had met each other . . . under mysterious circumstances—circumstances that they sometime later confessed were AA meetings.

I have recently discovered this last impression is indeed correct. A friend told me that, at one of the groups she was attending, every time a new person came in, the others would turn and look at this new person with the gleam of possibility in their eyes—and a little drool on their lips. When it became evident to my friend that they were spending far more time processing the ever-shifting tides of coupledom in the group than they were on what *she* thought the topic was supposed to be—staying sober—she left the group. Ah those lesbians—you can lead them to water, but you still can't get them to talk about drinking! I don't imagine, of course, that all lesbian AA groups are like that, and yet. . . . When you put a group of attractive women together, all in one room, sharing their most intimate thoughts and problems, bonds are bound to form.

As for myself, and why I've never learned the secret handshake of a 12-step group, well, it actually makes a certain amount of sense: I'm not an adult child of alcoholics and I'm not an abuser of either alcohol or drugs. You might think this is because I don't have a particularly addictive personality. True, but it also has something to do with what was so aptly phrased on a bumper sticker many years ago as "Reality is for people who can't handle drugs." In other words, I always felt like I had sort of a tenuous hold on reality at best and I didn't want to risk doing anything to mess that up. In the long run, I guess this has turned out for the best. But there was a time when such a drug-free stance was definitely not cool. Which is why I think those wrestling with an addiction problem are even more admirable.

But even if there were a 12-step program for overwriters anonymous or adult children of couch potatoes, I'm not sure I'd go. I don't mean to imply that these programs don't help a lot of people. On the contrary, I've seen evidence that they do. I'm just not very good at group confession. Personally, I like to embarrass the hell out of myself one person at a time—like with you right now, reading this book.

This same embarrassment factor has caused me to be hesitant about going to a lesbian therapist, someone who hangs out in the same community that I do, who knows some of the same people I do. I know they're sworn to secrecy and all, but I still think it would be awkward to see one's therapist socially. I'd be thinking to myself, *Why is she smiling like that? Is that an "Oh, poor thing" smile? Or a "I can't believe the things I know about you that all these other people don't" smile?* It's bad enough, at parties and concerts, to run into your ex-lovers, who know way too much about you—stuff that could be astoundingly embarrassing—but at least with your ex-lovers, you know plenty of potentially mortifying stuff about them too. This creates a nice system of checks and balances that helps keep people morally upright. Generally, one does not have such reciprocal knowledge of one's therapist. I have weighed these cons of having a lesbian therapist against the pros—having someone who understands lesbian culture without having to consult her copy of *The Well of Loneliness*—and so far, I have decided to throw my lot in with the hetero women who show me their breasts and videotape me for posterity. But that's just me. Therapy, of course, is a different experience for everyone—though my experience, perhaps, has been more different than most! I'm seeing a new one on Monday. I'm bringing along some balloons, just in case I spot that helium tank.

Ransacking The Closet

Coming out is like housework: just when you think you're done with it, it's time to do it again.

One of the most popularly asked questions in the lesbian community—next to, Do you really think Katarina Witt is a lesbian?—is, When did you come out? *Which time?* Sometimes, we lesbians have to come out to *ourselves* several times, not to mention to the thousands of other people nationwide who are absolutely riveted by the question of our sexuality. The when-did-you-come-out question, of course, actually translates roughly to, When did you figure out why you were more drawn to Ralph on *Green Acres* than to her brother?

As for my own experience, if I had been paying attention at all, there were about a million signs that I was a lesbian in the making. But the truth of it is, for a neurotically introspective person, I can often be quite dense about some very fundamental aspects of my life. Some would call this "denial." Personally, I just think of it as being "slow on the uptake"—but maybe I'm simply in denial about being in denial. I'm not quite sure because, when *I* was doing all my bulk-loading of therapy, it was pre all this New Age psycho-lingo—before everyone got so damn sensitive and spiritual about everything. In the old days, either your mind was warped or it wasn't. Period.

In any case, this lack of insight about myself has caused me a certain amount of cognitive dissonance: How could I, a self-proclaimed self-analytical type, miss these salient details about myself and my life? Until a few years ago, I didn't even know I had a giant freckle on my left ear! My girlfriend knew—even Flo and Rubynn at work knew—but I hadn't ever realized it was there until one day, much to my surprise, I noticed it while looking in the mirror.

Oh, I know: the ear is pretty much external and not the internal sort of thing to which I have been alluding here, but that should give you some idea of how deep this problem goes with me. To give another example at a more introspective level: it wasn't until I attended a program on class issues around 1981 that I first realized I was from a working-class background. It's beyond me now—having grown up in housing projects with a family that held down jobs like clerk typist, linotype machinist, heat treater, and short-order cook—how I was able to think of myself as being from a middle-class family.

So. Unlike friends who claim that since, like, age three or something they knew they were lesbians (I don't think I even knew I was *human* at age three), I didn't have so much as a glimmering that I was a lesbian until sometime in high school, and even then I rather successfully avoided knowledge of that knowledge. Still, given the huge blind spot I seem to have when it comes to insight about myself, I thought it might be useful to look more closely for signs of budding baby dykehood. So, like Danny Dunn, time traveler, hero of one of my favorite book series when I was a kid, I am journeying back in time. If you close your eyes, you can see the big swirling spiral taking us there. I see myself wearing bell bottoms, a vinyl vest, a shiny shirt with a big pointy collar, and a really bad haircut—either the spiral is spinning too fast or it must be high school.

My first clue that I wasn't your average hetero high schooler should have been the fact that, as a junior, rather than being crushed out on a member of the football team—or anyone else ever known to wear a jockstrap, for that matter—the object of my innocent desires was an older woman. A senior. And then, of course, there was Miss Kaufman. Miss Kaufman of the big brown eyes and lustrous brown hair. Miss Kaufman of second-year French. Miss Kaufman—or Cindy, as I liked to think of her privately—who once told me that I was too intense and frightened people. Yeah, I'll bet—like her, for instance!

Going back to junior high, I suspect I've unearthed more evidence: my padded-vinyl scrapbook, with the cover illustration of a ponytailed, be-loafered teen talking on the phone surrounded by a stack of 45s. Yep: that was me to a tee—NOT. But what was it that I found to grace the pages of my own private zine? The Fab Four? The Prefab Four (commonly known as The Monkees)? Or even Bobby Sherman? Nope. None of those guys. My pages were filled with the ever-popular Connie Stevens and an occasional photo of Nancy Sinatra in those famous boots. I'm sure my mother thought it was just a phase.

Also from junior high: when all the other girls were dreaming of getting their own ponies, I wanted an iguana, and got one. I dreamt of him growing to be three feet long and of taking him for walks in the neighborhood—oh, wait a minute: that just proves I was *weird*, not that I was a lesbian.

Okay, the iguana was not a tremendously good point of evidence. But what about this? In the years preceding junior high school, when all the other girls on my block were rabidly fantasizing in their own little prepubescent way with the help of Barbie and Ken, my own dolls were gathering dust in the closet. And on those occasions when peer pressure prevailed, I found that my dolls always wanted to go off by twos—say, Barbie and Midge—into the seclusion of the wilderness. It seems clear to me now that I was acting out the story of *Patience and Sarah* about fifteen or twenty years before it was published. As a child, you see, I was—surprisingly enough—your proverbial tomboy. I dreamt of being Tarzan or Boy, never Jane; I preferred *Treasure Island* to *Little Women;* I wanted my own skateboard and played marbles, not jacks: I won second place in the softball throw in fifth grade, for god's sake! How much of an indication does a person need?

Even before this there were clues. As special as Miss Kaufman and Connie Stevens were, neither was the first to lay claim to my rapidly beating heart. Before them came Miss Armstrong (her name, I think, speaks for itself) in third grade, whom I've always remembered as having a special affection for me. Hmmm. Anyway, prior to her was my uncle's first wife, who looked like Faye Dunaway. Maybe that's why I've always had such a fondness for that scene in *Little Big Man* where she bathes Dustin Hoffman. . . . Even Faye, though—I mean Aunt Karen—was not the first. Preceding her was Pippi Longstocking, with her red pigtails sticking straight out to the side and her habit of sleeping with her head at the foot of the bed and her feet on the pillows. All I can say is, thank god one's taste in women changes over the years.

With the weight of all this evidence, you'd think I would have figured out before some time in college that I was a lesbian. Even then, I was awfully slow. Take that day, one summer midway through college, when I found myself mashing my body up against a fellow camp counselor in a way I couldn't have named then but that scared the bejeezus out of me anyway. I jumped up off the bed and said accusingly to this woman, with whom I had been engaging in passionate and thoroughly naive verbal exchanges all summer: "I know what's going on here!" No doubt she did too—until that moment when I stunned her with my perversely outraged response to what must have seemed like a purely logical progression of things to her. All that book learnin', and I still couldn't figure out I was a lesbian!

Curiously enough, it was in a seminar at the university that I finally got a handle on my sexuality. Who says you can't get a good education at a state school? Actually, it wasn't anything the professor said or did or had us read. It was a fellow student who opened my eyes. She was butch and brash and crude and she always referred to her lover as her "old lady." She scared the hell out of me. Still, she never shut up about being a lesbian and so I couldn't help but ponder it. By the end of the semester, I found myself thinking, "Well, maybe I am a lesbian—and so what if I am?" I think some of her militancy must have rubbed off on me. Okay, so I was only confronting myself—but I was doing it belligerently.

With this revelation, a whole lot of things started falling in place. Aha! *That's* why I never felt anything, other than disgust maybe, when Darrell planted a big slobbery kiss on me. Well, okay, it was either the lesbian thing or the fact that he blew his nose, unaided by tissue or handkerchief, directly onto the street. It was a freeing experience—the realizing I was a lesbian, not the blowing of one's nose onto the street, although I've never tried it, so who am I to knock it?—freeing, that is, never to have to worry again that I was getting better grades than some guy or that I was beating the pants off him, so to speak, at pinball. Being a lesbian meant never having to worry about looking "feminine" enough, something I had always had trouble with no matter how foofy the dress. I always felt like I was in drag, like people could just *look* at me and *see* I didn't belong in any darn *dress*.

And speaking of dresses, when you first come out to yourself it's a lot like being all dressed up with no place to go. What I mean is, what's the fun of being a lesbian if you're the only one? Of course you're not *literally* the only one, but you might as well be if you don't know where the rest of 'em are! Other than the woman from my seminar (who already had an old lady, as you may recall), I knew of no lesbians in the entire city of Milwaukee and knew nowhere I might look to find them. Stonewall may have happened in New York, but here in the heartland, "stone wall" was still pretty much something you'd expect to find on a farm.

That's why I resorted to the fall-in-love-first, ask-questions-later method. Lucky for me, the object of my affections didn't flee screaming in terror when I revealed to her that not only was I pretty sure I was a lesbian but I thought I was falling in love with her as well. Eventually, after she got used to the idea, we actually got involved and were together for several years. However, the trial and error approach *can* be dangerous, messy, and, worst of all, embarrassing. Fortunately, there are more resources available these days for kids who are just coming out. Even so, it's still tough to find others like yourself.

I began contemplating this difficulty anew one day when my gal and I were watching a news show on TV. There was an item about Dr. Kevorkian, or "Dr. Death," as he has come to be known. The latter appellation causes me to confuse him with some fat bald-headed guy who used to be on All-Star Wrestling when I was a kid, and then I always think how nice it is that he got skinny, got hair, and got a medical degree. Most of those wrestling guys pretty much let themselves go after their glory days of jumping on people's heads and wedging them into the ropes.

Anyway, the news-show people talked to some right-to-life babe who looked like she had borrowed Mrs. Cleaver's wardrobe for the occasion and had gone to the same hairdresser Jackie O. frequented during her first lady days. I know this will surprise you, but Mrs. Right-to-Life was decidedly anti-Kevorkian. She explained her position something like this: "We have to put a stop to this or before you know it, suicide centers will be springing up right next to the abortion mills." "Those must be right down the road from the gay and lesbian recruitment centers," piped in my ever-helpful girlfriend.

Recruitment centers, I thought—what a great idea. Anita Bryant said years ago that we recruited new gays and lesbians, and all sorts of right-wing and red-necked kooks have always believed her, so why not go with it and set up an actual recruitment center? Right there in the strip mall, you'd have your army recruiter, your navy recruiter, your air force recruiter—and your gay recruiter and your lesbian recruiter—two separate offices because, really, they are two very different branches of the service. One defends this great country of ours from its stations in the opera houses, the other from the softball fields. The more I thought about it, the more I warmed to the idea. "Be all you can be: Join the lesbians." "It's not just a job, it's an adventure." And of course, the all too obvious: "Looking for a few good men."

So, to return to my earlier point: among the biggest problems still confronting gay and lesbian kids today are *(1)* not knowing they're not alone in their queerness and *(2)* not knowing where to find others like themselves. With our recruitment centers set up right there next to Pudgy's Red Hots and Dunkin' Donuts, how could they miss us? We could solve both of their problems in one fell swoop. There could be giant posters in the windows showing healthy red-blooded lesbians, doing lesbian things—kissing another woman, engaging in civil disobedience, or maybe both at the same time if there wasn't a lot of poster room—so the kids would see what an active fulfilling life they could have and would want to come on in to find out more.

Once inside, a vibrant specimen of lesbianhood would greet them and tell them all the great things about being a lesbian: being on the inside track when new concepts are born, like the use of a fanny pack as a purse; going on the Oprah show with a label under your name that says "Hates men"; serial monogamy; becoming instantly chic; and, of course, not having to pore over *Consumer Reports,* trying to figure out which condom to buy. The recruiter would tell them how being a lesbian is a defining experience for most women who enlist—and how some even become career lesbians, like Kate Clinton and Urvashi Vaid.

Then, the potential recruit would be treated to a film about lesbian boot camp: the Michigan Womyn's Music Festival. This could possibly scare off a few of the more faint-hearted who don't know if they're woman enough to handle (so to speak) all those bare breasts, but maybe they're just not ready yet. In which case, the recruiter would tell them the door is always open if they change their minds. Why, they could even join up with the lesbians, quit, and then reenlist. Hey! It's been known to happen.

Once the new recruit *has* decided this is just the thing for her, it's time to make that all-important decision of whether to specialize or not. Does she want to become a lipstick lesbian? A crunchy dyke? A Queer Nation member? A jock? The choice made at this juncture would of course determine what sort of uniform would be issued and where the recruit would be told to report. In most cases, of course, the best plan is to delay choosing a specialty and just enjoy the basic training—hitting the bars and hanging out at the women's coffeehouse, meeting the girl of her dreams, moving in with her—and breaking up. Listen—no one ever said being a baby dyke was *easy*.

Next door there in the strip mall, the recruitment center for gay men would be a lot like this one, with pretty much the same areas of specialization offered, only instead of "lipstick lesbian" it would be "drag queen." It would be different, though, from the lesbian center in that the furniture would be classier and the recruitment speech would place a lot more emphasis on grooming. Also, as far as I know, other than for the S/M guys, there is no boot camp.

Maybe, if there was some sort of crisis—like Jesse Helms got *really* out of control or we didn't have enough women to form a softball team one year—we could institute a draft. Personally, I would like to draft Mary Stuart Masterson, Emma Thompson, Carol Moseley Braun, and Janet Reno, though not all necessarily for the same reasons. Whether these particular women were selected by the draft board would depend, of course, on whether or not they had, without my knowledge, already joined up.

Okay—so maybe drafting women to fill my own personal fantasy "army" is getting a little off track from my point. Returning to it, I would like to assert that the recruitment centers could definitely help someone ease her way into the lesbian community. And yet, really, the hard part isn't coming out to other lesbians. That's a little like confessing to a priest that you go to mass everyday. No, the ones who are tough to confess to are those folks who aren't known to you to be practicing lesbians—and the list of unverified lesbians seems dauntingly endless. There are your parents, your siblings, your coworkers, your neighbors, your doctors, your dentist, your dog groomer, your teammates, your grandparents, and the kid who takes your order at McDonald's, for starters. You don't have to come out to every last one of them, of course, but if you wanted to, a very efficient way to do it would be to get involved in a Queer Nation action in which you chain yourself to City Hall or participate in a kiss-in in the middle of an intersection downtown. That way, you get yourself on the ten o'clock news, and boom:

you're done. You've just effectively come out to everyone you know. Not that all of your viewers are necessarily going to consider this *good* news. . . .

The thing of it is, I have found it very hard to predict who will and who won't. My grandmother, for instance, who is not particularly known for her tolerance of those unlike herself, barely batted an eye when I came out to her. She has more trouble with my being a *vegetarian* than with my being a lesbian. She is very conscientious about recognizing my relationship with Kathy, never failing to enquire after her health and always sending her love. My uncle, on the other hand, a relatively young, hip, and groovin' kind of guy, has never once uttered the word "lesbian" in my hearing and doesn't know my, uh, *friend*'s name—even though Kathy and I have *owned a house together* longer than either of his first two marriages lasted.

Though my uncle and his third wife are clearly uncomfortable with the whole homosexuality thing, no one in my family has disowned me. Other people I know have been cut off completely from their families—some people have all the luck! But seriously, for those who actually *like* their families—and their jobs—coming out is an anxiety-producing situation at best: there is so much to lose.

That's why, a number of years ago, I came up with a sort of alternative plan, trial runs, if you will—the "hit-and-run coming out"—in which you come out to virtual strangers: store clerks, health care technicians, fellow seminar attendees, etc. It is probably not, on the other hand, a particularly good idea to come out at random to all the guys down at Bronco Billy's Red-neck Saloon and Shooting Range or to the passengers sharing an el car with you at 2 a.m. Once you have selected the appropriate folks, the beauty of a hit-and-run coming out is that you declare your lesbianism to someone else's relative, coworker, or friend—with little hazard to yourself—hopefully paving the way for some other nervous dyke. What's more, it gives you much needed practice, helps open up a few more minds (even if it's only an eensy bit), fights lesbian invisibility, breaks down stereotypes, and cuts through waxy build-up to reveal your floor's natural shine. Well, okay: maybe not that last. But such kamikaze comings out, heart-rate-raising as they can be, do actually accomplish an awful lot.

Besides, aren't you tired of having to act coy when the old guy at the shoe repair shop teases you about all the boyfriends you must have? Tired of changing your pronouns when chatting about your personal life with the folks in your ceramics class? Of being evasive when the X-ray technician asks, for the second or third time, "Are you *sure* you're not pregnant?" Wouldn't it be satisfying to say, "Yes, I'm sure. I'm a lesbian. If I were pregnant, I'd damn well know it!" Of course, you might not want to say this to the woman who is giving you a mammogram just as she's putting your breast in that vice: you don't want to risk giving her any kind of shock that might cause her to crank the thing a notch too tight. . . .

Of course, eventually, you are probably going to have to come out to people you know. Even if you suspect the other person might be a lesbian, it's not always easy. Because what if you're wrong about her? At least with someone you think is a lesbian, there are ways of easing into self-revelation through casual conversation. When you mention, for instance, going to Michigan in August, does she say, "Oh, I hear it's lovely there that time of year." Or does she ask whether you usually camp in the Twilight Zone or Jupiter Jump Off? Is her favorite cartoonist Alison Bechdel? Or Kathy Guisewite? When you're talking about country and western music, at the mention of k. d. lang does she mutter, "That damn weirdo," or does she sigh wistfully and blush? At a certain point, after some number of these conversational cake testers, you don't have to worry about coming out: you already have.

There are certainly ways of dropping clues about your sexuality to your parents too. Like moving back and forth across the country four or five times with the same woman. Or buying a house with a woman and living there with her for ten or twenty years. Or wearing to Christmas dinner a "Power Lunch" t-shirt with the two women engaging in oral sex. But I have found that parents often have elaborate systems of denial wedged firmly in place—how else do you think so many of them are able to stay married to each other?—and are capable of ignoring evidence as blatant as your blind devotion to your women's recreational softball team or the fact that you haven't mentioned a man's name besides your brother's since Dennis stuck the frog head on his pencil in tenth-grade biology. Then there's nothing left to do but just blurt it out. Sometimes even then I don't think they quite believe. A lot of parents cling very tightly to the "it's just a phase" hope, apparently unfazed by the fact that you are now forty and this stage you are going through has lasted about a quarter of a century. The only thing remaining to do at that point is have your parents walk in on you while you're making love with another woman.

There is, of course, a viable alternative to coming out: remaining in the closet. This I can offer no advice on, being an abject failure at it myself. I think I kind of sort of used to be able to do it years ago, but since I have become at one with my lesbianism, I no longer recognize which are my lesbian parts and so I don't know what to hide. But I suspect the gals who are still in the closet aren't, for the most part, all that good at it either. Take your corporate dyke—have you ever seen one of those gals walking in heels? Harvey Fierstein in drag does a better job of looking feminine than some of them.

The only reason the closet thing seems to work, I think, is because the closet case and her hetero henchpeople are in cahoots together: she doesn't want them to know and they don't want to know. They are her co-closeters—the ultimate codependents. The way it works is, whatever she hasn't covered up very well, the rest of them just ignore or explain away. "It's so *practical* of her to have purchased that house with that other woman. Sure they go everywhere together—a woman alone just can't be *safe* anymore. I think it's great, too, how active she is for a grown woman—I hear she plays on both a basketball *and* a softball team."

The closet, of course—and when and how to get the hell out of it—are very complex and personal issues. In my case, though, it was pretty much just a matter of time before I'd come bursting out. You see, I am afflicted with uncontrollable congenital honesty. To put it another way, when I say to you that I am a terrible liar, I don't mean that I do it a lot; I mean I do it very badly. If I even *think* about lying, I start to sweat, develop a stutter and an eye twitch, and grow so warm that, what with the sweat and all, steam starts to rise off of my body—all of which adds tons of credibility to anything I then utter. To avoid this sensation of discovering what it might be like to burn in hell (which I'm not even sure I believe in), I instead simply blurt out The Truth, no matter how compromising the situation—much to the frustration of my girlfriend, who was raised Catholic and therefore received ample training in the fine art of lying.

It is not only my affliction that causes me to announce to all and sundry the fact that I'm a lesbian. It is also that I am just pleased as punch to *be* a lesbian (the pay is lousy, but the benefits are great) and want to share the good news of my lesbianism with whoever will listen. Whoa: I think I just channeled Billy Graham there. For me, when it comes to being a lesbian, it's like experiencing episodes of Tourette's syndrome: I can't shut up about it, already. I'm afraid I am eternally condemned to a life outside the closet. But if you could see the stacks of boxes, the basket of old shoes, the abandoned space heater, and the articles of clothing spanning as many as three decades currently occupying my closet, you would know, as I do, that this is an especially propitious thing.

Coda:

Or, The Last Laugh?

Now that you know everything there is to know about lesbians, what are you planning to do? Well, if you're thinking of going to Disneyland like a winning quarterback, hold off on packing those bags for a bit. Because of course no single book could capture all there is to the lesbian world. We lesbians just come in too darn many varieties, like mongrel pups. With attitudes. And even though I like to think of myself as Every Lesbian, to assert that I am, in fact, the prototypical lesbian is a little like saying that Groucho Marx was representative of the 1940s American male or that Roseanne is your average housewife of the 1990s.

Still, I like to believe the picture of lesbian life I have drawn shows us to be not only human but downright lovable as well. I ask you, What could be more lovable than a dyke wearing wire-rim glasses and a homespun-type jumper, wielding a laptop computer? Maybe one in chaps sporting a whip and a wicked grin. But I guess that's a matter of preference. Which, when you think about it, is pretty much the raison d'être of this book: matters of preference, both grand and tiny.

What am I going to do, now that I've written everything I know about lesbians? Heck, I haven't even scratched the surface of what I know! And by the time I get all *that* down on paper, it will have changed anyway. So basically, I have my life's work cut out for me: Y. Zipter, documenter of dykes, Esq. Who knew, when I came out those many years ago, that I was making not only a "lifestyle" choice but a career choice as well? Fortunately for me, it is indeed not just a job but an adventure.

So I haven't quite earned that trip to Disneyland yet either. But when I do go, I will be certain to look up my role model there. And although comedian Marga Gomez, impersonating Anaïs Nin, does make Minnie Mouse, with her two rows of hard little nipples, sound like quite the rodent goddess, it is not Ms. Mouse I will seek out. No, my own personal Disney soulmate would have to be Goofy. Hm: Do you suppose it's a problem that I share a worldview with a dim-witted cartoon character dog? But you have to admit: the two of us, we sure do know how to enjoy a good laugh.

Afterword:

Who's Responsible For This?

Depending on one's view of the contents of this book, the following people are owed blame or thanks. (Although surely they could not be held responsible for my waywardness in a court of law?) Regardless of the reader's position, I am nothing but grateful to each and all. To begin at a point that could be construed as the beginning, I feel compelled to point out Tracy Baim, who nudged me, way back in 1985, toward writing the column from which this book sprang forth and also for giving me unconditional writing space—which for a writer is almost the same thing as unconditional love.

Next in line is my agent, Julie Fallowfield, and her associate, Louise Quayle, who had faith in me and in this book, even when neither I nor various editors did. Also joining the queue is Syd Lea, who somehow managed to cheerlead at the same time he instructed—though I feel a little cheated that I never actually got to see his cheerleading outfit. Then there's Phyllis Barber, who held me accountable on several points and made the book better as a result. My editor, Kelly Kager, had the formidable task of tidying up after I had "ransacked the closet." Roger Weingarten graciously permitted me to do some of the work for this book in the context of my MFA in writing degree at Vermont College. Joining the ranks of the likes of these are Mary Leas and Robert Sherrill, who demonstrated the flexibility of Gumby in allowing me to rearrange my "day job" in a manner conducive to writing this book. My close friends Laura, Martha, Maureen, and Corinne, along with a legion of other lesbians, are responsible, whether they like it or not, for so much of the material contained herein. Thanks go, too, to all of my readers over the years, who let me know I made them laugh, though they may now regret it because, as I've said, it only encouraged me. And last on the page but first in my heart: my lover Kathleen Forde, whose presence in my life is evident in every chapter, every insight, every joke: thank you, love, for being the polka-dotted galluses of my soul: just the right mix of levity and support.

Yvonne Zipter is the author of the syndicated column “Inside Out,” the nonfiction book *Diamonds Are A Dyke’s Best Friend,* and the poetry collection *The Patience of Metal,* which was runner-up for the Poetry Society of America’s Melville Cane Award and a Lambda Literary Award Finalist.